EXPLORING
CANDLE MAGICK

Candle Spells, Charms, Rituals, and Divinations

EXPLORING
CANDLE MAGICK

Candle Spells, Charms, Rituals, and Divinations

Patricia Telesco

NEW PAGE BOOKS
A division of The Career Press, Inc.
Franklin Lakes, NJ

EXPLORING CANDLE MAGICK
Cover design by Diane Chin
Edited by Karen Prager
Typeset by Stacey A. Farkas
Illustrated by Colleen Koziara
Printed in the U.S.A. by Book-mart Press

To order this title, please call toll-free 1-800-CAREER-1 (NJ and Canada: 201-848-0310) to order using VISA or MasterCard, or for further information on books from Career Press.

The Career Press, Inc., 3 Tice Road, PO Box 687, Franklin Lakes, NJ 07417
www.careerpress.com
www.newpagebooks.com

Library of Congress Cataloging-in-Publication Data

Telesco, Patricia, 1960-
    Exploring candle magick : candle spells, charms, rituals, and divinations / by Patricia Telesco.
        p. cm.
    Includes bibliographical references and index.
    ISBN 1-56414-522-0
    1. Candles and lights—Miscellanea. 2. Magic. I. Title.

BF1623.C26 T45 2001
133.4'3—dc21

00-065389

To all those I love—you are the lights of my life

Contents

Preface
A Light in the Darkness: Candles in History, Lore, and Aromatherapy

I shall light a candle of understanding in thine heart,
which shall not be put out.
—The Apocrypha

W hat would a romantic dinner for two be without candlelight? How sad would a birthday cake seem without candles? We think little of these things because candles are commonplace. Nonetheless, we are certainly not the first people to use them for everything from religious observances to special occasions, not to mention lighting.

Candle History in Brief

History is very sketchy about the candle's humble beginnings. It is suspected that in the farthest reaches of human history, animal fat was used to create pseudo candles to light the night and chase away any evil spirits lurking about. In written chronicles, candle holders dating to the fourth century B.C. have been found in Egypt, which indicates the likelihood of a much older origin date. Evidence also suggests that the Egyptians used tallow from suet as the main ingredient in candles. The Greeks and Romans seemed to follow suit, adding a handy wick to the construction.

The idea of fat-laden candles may seem odd to us, and rather messy, but fat is only one of the unusual ingredients to show up in candle-making's history. Others include:

- Wax gathered from insects and molded with seeds (Japan).
- Wax gathered from boiling cinnamon (India).
- Cerio tree wax (Southwestern U.S.).
- Bayberry wax (New England).
- Spermaceti from sperm whales (various locations).
- Candelilla leaves, esparto grass, palm leaf wax (various locations).
- Stormy petrel and candlefish (Pacific Northwest).

The word candle comes from a Latin term meaning "torch" or "to make bright." The symbolic value of the word and the candle's illumination wasn't lost on early theologians. The Catholic church began using a white candle to represent Christ's purity, God's power, and spiritual awareness around 5 A.D.

Something resembling modern candles started to appear around the 1200s. This is when we see the first dipped tapers made from tallow and beeswax. Beeswax was by far preferable in both appearance and smell, but it was also very expensive. So, for a while, beeswax candles became a sign of wealth. This was also about the time that color began to be added to candles.

Around this same time candle-maker guilds were well established. One guild was specifically for those who made candles from animal fat, and another group made them from beeswax. In Paris, the guilds were taxed for candle production, which is a pretty good indication that business was booming.

Candle-molding techniques followed in the 1400s, making candles more accessible to the general public. With this change in the industry, governments looked for more ways to profit from this ancient device. Meanwhile, in the late 1500s, the Catholic church began using red candles at mass because it seemed to improve the impact of sermons on those in attendance.

Come the 17th century, the English banned homemade candles, requiring people to buy a license to make them, and then pay taxes on the candles produced! In the 18th century European governments were often regulating the size, weight, and price of candles. By the 1800s candle-making machines were born, along with the first matches, and by 1850 candle crafters were using paraffin.

Meanwhile, across the sea in America, people were presenting gifts of candles to newlyweds so that the couple would never want, and as a wish for many children. Since that time the world of candlecraft has been something of an open book. Commercial candle companies have sprung up around the world, offering candles in every color and shape imaginable. And thanks to books and classes on the subject, many individuals have also taken up the art as a pastime in recent years. All this is very good news for the magickal practitioners who want to have variety and/or the option of making candles from scratch to saturate them with personal energy.

Superstitions and Beliefs

I firmly believe that many magickal practices hid themselves under the safe, and more socially acceptable, veneer of folklore and superstition in many settings. This is especially true during the years when magick and witchcraft were taboos, and people feared for their lives. After all, most people don't blink at a superstitious act that's been repeated for generations...and they hardly think it magickal. Upon further investigation, however, the imprint of magick abounds in many of these beliefs. Here are just a few of the superstitions surrounding candles:

Luck and Blessings:

- Always light a candle with your right hand for good fortune. If the candle should go immediately out, however, bad luck will follow. This belief could easily be adapted to a candle spell for luck!

- Never singe the base of a candle to make it fit firmly. This brings misfortune. So, for ritual and spellcraft it might be a better idea to melt wax into the container and then place the candle within so it's secure.

- Allow Yule candles to burn out naturally for blessings and luck. Add this idea to your holiday celebrations.

- Never light three candles with one match, or have three candles burning together. This brings mishaps. This is one area where magick differs, as three is a sacred number to the Goddess and represents the triune nature of humankind.

- Only a woman named Mary should snuff the candles on Christmas day so the blessing isn't lost. This one isn't overly practical, but interesting!

❧ Give the gift of a bayberry candle on New Year's Eve to friends to whom you wish luck, prosperity, and health. Note that this should be burned completely on New Year's Eve for the greatest effect. This belief is perfect for magick just as it is.

Money:

❧ If you wish to grow rich, never light a candle from a burning fire. Use this as a guideline when working prosperity and money magick.

Protection:

❧ If it's storming outside, light a blessed candle for safety. Most magickal practitioners would likely use a white candle for this purpose, as white is the color of protection.

❧ Lighting a candle at a child's birth, after a death, and on one's birthday affords extra protection from evil. This is a great idea all the way around. At a birth ceremony, the light honors the spirit of the child coming into this world. At death, it shows the spirit the way out into the next incarnation. And on your birthday, a candle reminds you of your own light, which should always be honored.

Signs and Omens:

❧ A candle that goes out during a ritual indicates the presence of a restless ghost. Actually, I've often found this to be very true. If a spirit shows up at a ritual it will not, however, be able to enter the sacred circle without permission. Use your own discretion here, being aware that not all spirits are nice, nor do all of them have good intentions.

- In ancient Greece if a girl could blow on a candle flame and then re-spark it, she was marked as a vestal virgin and given the task of tending Vesta's sacred fires. Vesta is a fantastic goddess for a candle crafter to call upon for blessings in his or her art.

- Candles that burn blue or have wax that forms a winding sheet around the base reveal the presence of spirits. Alternatively some people consider this a death omen. In magick, watching the wax or flame of a candle is a common form of divination, and there are tons of meanings associated with a flame's movements, which will be covered later in this book.

- If a candle will not light, a storm is coming. This is actually true because of the dampness in the air.

- A candle sparking bright portends a letter for the person sitting across from it (see Chapter 2).

- Accidentally knocking a candle over and having it go out indicates a forthcoming marriage in the family (see Chapter 2).

- If a person can revive a sputtering candle it indicates he or she is virtuous and pure of heart (see Chapter 2).

- Seeing a ring in the candle flame indicates an engagement or marriage (see Chapter 2).

- A lump of soot on the wick of a candle reveals that a stranger will soon visit (see Chapter 2).

Wishes:

- The ritual of blowing out birthday candles may have originated with rites for Artemis. The key is blowing out all the candles at once. The smoke that follows carries your wishes to the heavens. This is a great bit of wishcraft that works wonderfully just as it is. Remember, however, that silence is power in this magick. Telling the wish dissipates the energy behind it.

Candles and Aromatherapy

Although it may seem odd to include aromatherapy in a section about history and superstition, the topics are intimately tied together. Historically, the use of aroma is well known in mysticism and religion. Ancient temple priests and priestesses burned incense, believing that the aroma pleased the gods and the smoke carried prayers to the heavens. The ancient Babylonians even went so far as to put perfume in the blocks that formed the temples, and in India many sacred spaces had sandalwood walls for much the same reason.

As early as 1500 B.C., healers were using aromatics like lavender to improve a patient's disposition and speed recovery. Egyptians used aromatics to treat depression, for example. In Greece, Hippocrates studied the effects of aromas on healing and concluded that scented baths or massages could be very beneficial to humankind.

And where did these people and others like them come by the applications for various aromas? Why, the folklore and mythology of the plants from which the aromas come, of course! Much of these myths and tales originated in Arabia, China, and India where investigating plant properties was quite common. This information, laden with magick, was then carried with clever traders via caravan around the known world. This, of course, also served to increase the price of the goods, as they had such wondrous powers.

Even with all this excitement, the actual "science" of aromatherapy didn't begin to form until the late 1920s. It's interesting, however, that many of the ancient correspondences for aromas remained: lavender for peace, lemon and clove for cleansing, and so forth. This means that the magickal candle maker has a lot of options from which to choose in considering the scent of a candle.

Here's a brief chart that you can use as a helpmate. Note that I have focused mostly on magickal aromatherapy associations here. In magickal aromatherapy, the scent released by burning the candle changes the vibrations in and around a person's aura, which in turn supports whatever magickal work he or she is doing if the aroma is chosen correctly.

Apple: Health, joy.

Berry: Good fortune, abundance, happiness.

Cedar: Cleansing, courage, purification.

Chamomile: Coping with life changes.

Cinnamon: Energy, improved appetite.

Frankincense: Blessings, decreasing anxiety.

Ginger: Power, settling the spirit.

Grapefruit: Refreshment, lifting despondency.

Honeysuckle: Prosperity, psychic awareness, safety.

Jasmine: Attracting a man, improving meditative focus.

Lavender: Rest, peace.

Lemon: Tonic quality, cleansing.

Lilac: Harmony, mental awareness.

Lotus: Spirituality, enlightenment.

Mint: Money, rejuvenation.

Myrrh: Banishing, turning spells, healing.

Orange: Improving sleep, tonic quality.

Patchouli: Keeping away insects (actual or figurative).

Peach: Wish fulfillment, wisdom, longevity.

Peppermint: Decreasing mental stress.

Pineapple: Welcome, hospitality.

Rose: Balancing feminine energies, love, friendship.
Rosemary: Memory retention.
Sage: Cleansing, wisdom.
Sandalwood: Self-confidence, spirituality.
Thyme: Fairy magick, psychism.
Vetiver: Transformation, shapeshifting, attracting a woman.

A common question that comes up at this point is where exactly does one get the scents for candles and how do you add them? I'll cover this issue in detail in Chapter 1. For now, suffice it to say that you can make your own aromatics or buy them, and adding scents to candles is incredibly simple, so don't sweat it!

Bear in mind that this list is only a starting point. You can rely on common aromatherapy correspondences, look to the metaphysical associations for the plant from which an aroma came, or just follow personal vision. There is no right or wrong here, save what makes sense to you and what seems to best support your spiritual goals.

ৡৡৡ

So there you have it, all wrapped up in wax! No matter where one looks, it seems that candles have been shining into human affairs, from those of state to those of spirit, for a very long time. We are now simply going to take candle-lighting to a different level, one with will, purpose, and perfect love as a guide.

Introduction

For as long as we live, our path will be lit like the flame of the candle. Our home will shelter and protect us so the flame will burn ever bright and warm.
—Holly L. Rose, *Where the Heart Is*

A woman stands gazing thoughtfully across an old wooden table. Crystals, a pewter chalice, a large feather, some sage incense, and a seashell have been carefully placed upon it to create a circle. In the center, the point of this simple mandala and altar, lies one pure, white candle. The woman breathes deeply, focusing the mind and will into harmony, reaches gently across, and lights the taper. The magick has begun.

No, this isn't a description of a movie scene or a play. In fact, these types of activities are happening every day, enacted by people just like you and me—people who want to ignite the flame of real magick in their daily lives. And in the center of all this spiritual activity we discover an ancient symbol and tool: a simple candle.

There is something special and truly magickal about candlelight. It creates an ambiance that feels different. Cloaked in the gentle glow of the candle, it's easier to put our nine-to-five world aside and think about mystical things. In the flickers of that flame we can almost hear the whispers of ancient times, times when magick was no more "supernatural" than birthing babies. These whispers call to us and beg us to listen and follow that simple, yet wise, example.

Throughout the world candles have been part of religious ceremonies, representing the presence of Spirit and the spiritual light that lives in each human being. In many forms of folk magick, candles play a role in divination, either as the tool for fortune telling, as a focal point, or as a means of changing the mood. In Wicca, Strega, Santeria, and many other mystical traditions, candles are an integral part of spellcraft and ritual.

Why the popularity? Probably because candles were nearly always available and easy to make. Our ancestors were a pragmatic lot who looked at everyday items and the world around them as a readily accessible source of magickal components. After all, they didn't have the local superstore to turn to when various items ran out! Along the same lines, when one thing wasn't on hand, another meaningful one got substituted. This is how candles came to be everything from poppets to enchanted pomades.

Blend all this history together and you have a pretty impressive foundation on which to build a whole school around candle magick. It could easily be said that if you choose no other tools for magick, you'd at least want a candle. They are, in fact, the tool that I favor above everything else, except myself.

So where does one begin? From my perspective, it's easiest to start at the beginning—the history and lore of candles. These chronicles and superstitions house an abundance of magick sprinkled liberally throughout, some traditions of which remain to this very day.

Using this as a foundation, *Exploring Candle Magick* goes on to explore candle crafts. Candle-making isn't difficult, expensive, or overly time-consuming. What's more, I truly believe that people who make their own candles will achieve greater success magickally because of the personal energy that goes into the creation process.

Next, we'll look at candle scrying and other divination techniques, candles as amulets and charms, and candles in spellcrafting and ritual. These focal points represent the most common uses for candles throughout magickal practices. But I'm not done yet!

Taking this one step further, *Exploring Candle Magick* will review holidays that revel in candles. This, in turn, gives you the perfect opportunity to put some of your newly learned arts and crafts to work. There's also an appendix of gods and goddesses that have somehow been associated with candles so that, if you choose, you can call on appropriate powers to bless your efforts.

Last, but not least, we will talk about electric lighting. Why? Because this is the modern version of a candle, and because not every home or setting is suited to candlelight magick, this is a viable option for techno-witches everywhere. This section will give a whole new meaning to the phrase "light up your life."

As with any of my books, I strongly urge you to use your own discretion in what you take from these pages and apply to your life. My spiritual "light" is but one among many, and your heart should be the truest guru you have for magick. If anything here doesn't feel right, don't use it.

On the other hand, I believe that candle magick doesn't come across as hocus-pocus because this art has been with us for so long and has been used by so many who have walked this path before. *Exploring Candle Magick* is a celebration of this time-honored method as one that can easily adapt to anyone's spiritual vision. So turn the page, light the candles, and reclaim the night!

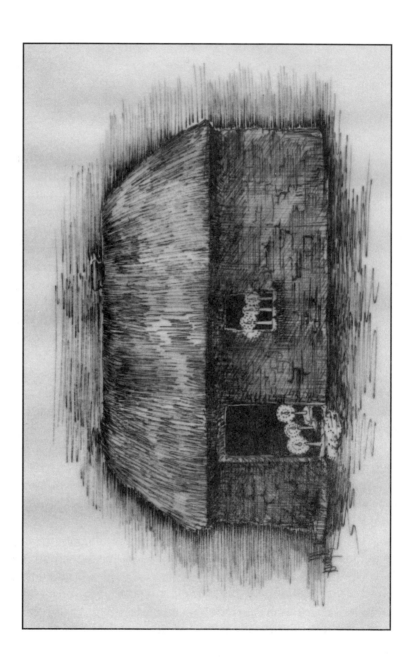

Candlecraft 101

Hope, like the gleaming taper's light, adorns and cheers our way.
—Oliver Goldsmith

I am a great advocate of reclaiming arts that have been lost to dusty bookshelves or technological advances. There is something special about items made by hand, a uniqueness and feel that you just can't get from machine crafts. From a spiritual standpoint, there is also a kind of energy that handmade items bear like a fingerprint. This astral fingerprint not only indicates who made the item, but for what type of magick it was made.

With this in mind, this chapter will review some of the simpler methods of making candles yourself. There are certainly more approaches than what I cover here, but I've chosen the ones that I feel will save readers the most time and cost the least in tools and materials. After all, we live in a time-challenged environment where scheduling doesn't always allow for long, drawn-out processes. If you're interested in more elaborate approaches to candle-making, there are some excellent books on the subject listed in the suggested reading list at the end of this book.

Secondly, this chapter discusses the magickal aspects of candle-making—namely how to instill a candle with the right energy for the task you have in mind. There are many things that you can easily do while making your candle that will have a positive effect on its completed symbolic value. Better still, following these techniques yields an item that, from beginning to end, was willfully fashioned for metaphysical use. This, in turn, results in more powerful and meaningful magick.

The Mundane Fundamentals

Okay, first the nitty-gritty. You can't add magick into a process if you have no idea where the process starts! I think many people reading this remember making milk carton candles at camp or school, and that's probably the extent to which most folks have been exposed to this ancient art. Heck, I have a lot of craft-oriented hobbies and I was totally taken back by the variety of candle-making methods and decorating techniques available. So, let's explore together!

A Sticky Wicket?

When buying a wick at a craft shop you'll notice that it's labeled for the size candle in which it can be used most successfully. Extra small candles are less than 1 inch in diameter, small ones are up to 2 inches in diameter, medium up to 3 inches, large up to 4 inches, and extra large continue upward from a 4-inch diameter.

You may also see other labels on the wicks. A flat braid wick is best for dipped and pillar candles. Square braids work well with beeswax, pillar candles, square block candles, and . novelty shapes. Cored wicks have support, which makes them ideal for self-contained candles. Note that no matter which wicks you choose, the strand must be soaked with wax for at least one minute, then pulled straight and allowed to cool. Then a small metal piece should be secured around one end (called a tab) before using it to make a candle. This tab goes in the bottom of the candle.

If a candle overflows its edge with wax, drowns in wax, or smokes a lot, you've chosen a wick that's too small. A wick that gathers carbon on the top, or a pillar candle that begins dripping out, indicates too large a wick. Candles that sputter may have air pockets and aren't very safe. It's best to re-melt and remold.

In researching this book I found it interesting that not all wicks are present in the pouring process. Some are inserted into a candle after it sets. This is done by using a thin, heated metal rod inserted through the candle, followed by threading the wick through that hole. Any excess space is then filled with additional wax. The advantage to this method is that you don't have to go crazy trying to keep the wick straight or erect while pouring molten wax.

Waxing and Waning:

Speaking of wax, there are also several kinds of wax, suited to different types of candles. A low melting point wax is best for self-contained candles and pillar candles so the wick can get more oxygen, for example. Other kinds of wax best suited to home candle-making efforts include:

- Bayberry: Very costly and hard to find, but makes a lovely scented candle (beware of paraffin that's scented with bayberry oil as this is *not* the same thing).

- Beeswax: A slow-burning wax whose color and aroma changes depending on the flowers from which the bees made it. More expensive than paraffin but also makes a longer lasting candle.

- Mix n' Match Wax: This is wax that you've saved from other candles. Although the results may be somewhat undependable, it's a great way to recycle and save money. Magickally, however, I suggest keeping candles that have been used for specific purposes together or carefully mixing, balancing, and matching the themes of the candles so the result isn't a lot of confusing energy.

- Paraffin: The most common wax used in modern candles. The advantage to paraffin is that it is separated by melting point. The disadvantage is that it needs to be mixed with 10 percent stearic acid to keep the wax hard and create an opaque appearance. Generally speaking you'll be looking for a melting point of 125 to 150 degrees and a fully refined paraffin, which is very dependable. Do not, however, buy paraffin at the supermarket. This doesn't make good candles (it's intended for canning).

Note that some candle makers blend waxes to create a variety of effects, like paraffin with beeswax and stearic acid for a good poured or dipped candle, or a 50-50 blend of paraffin and beeswax for molded candles. In any case, you need about

12 pounds of wax to make a dozen 10-inch long, 7/8-inch diameter taper candles (note that 1 1/2 cups of melted wax equals about one pound of solid wax). Generally speaking, it is best to buy wax at a craft supply store.

Additives:

For magickal candles it's highly likely that you'll wish to add herbs, oils, and other ingredients to personalize the energy. When you do, put in as little as possible and mix thoroughly. Bear in mind that wax with a high proportion of additive may not set or melt properly, let alone safely. In particular, make sure herbs are powdered (not in large pieces that can catch fire) and stir these into the liquid wax by hand for at least three to five minutes so they are evenly distributed.

Color:

Colored wax or color additives can be purchased at most craft supply stores. By far the most common is the aniline dyes that come with complete proportion instructions at your local craft store. A nice alternative for magickal candles, however, is looking to nature's storehouse for aid. This way there are no chemicals that might hinder the effective flow of energy.

Steep deeply colored flower, herb, or vegetable parts in warm wax, repeating as necessary to achieve the results desired. In particular beets yield a lovely red hue, fennel yields brown, onion skins give a pale brown or golden hue, and saffron gives a yellow.

Aromatics:

The easiest way to scent a candle is through essential or aromatherapy oils. I would avoid any aromatic that's decocted in alcohol, as it will lose its scent very quickly. Additionally, you may still have to rub the outside of the candle or dip the wick in more oil to get a personally pleasing level of potency. The average proportion of wax to oil is 1/2 pound of wax to 1/4 teaspoon oil. Under no circumstances should oil additives exceed 3 percent of the wax's weight.

Alternatively you can add powdered herbs and spices to the wax (or steep large plant parts in the wax) to create an aroma. Be careful, however, about the temperature at which you add the herbs. Some are heat sensitive (like roses) and need to wait until the wax is between hot and warm. This might mean repeated steeping, but it's far better than the smell of burnt plants!

Some of the best sources for aromatics are New Age stores, food cooperatives, spice and herb shops, and online sites such as *www.frontiercoop.com.*

Tools:

Like any craft, candle-making requires a few tools. If you choose to take these tools out of your home stock, do not return them to culinary use. Some of the additives for candle-making are not edible, so these tools should be safely stored away from kitchen utensils.

To begin, you need a pot. A non-aluminum double boiler is nice if you can find one, but otherwise a regular pan will do. A mixing spoon, ladle, newspaper (to cover the working surface), scissors, knife, paper clips or tape (to hold wick in place), plastic cutting board (for sheet wax), and bucket (to cool molds) are all easily found around the home. You'll also need pot holders and cold water. Wax gets very hot—upwards of 170 degrees at melting.

If your wax isn't already cut and weighed, you may need a scale. For candles that you plan to put a wick through after solidification, you'll want an ice pick or a metal rod that you can heat up. Finally, to make life easy, get some spray-on cooking oil so your candles come out of the mold easily.

Clean-Up Time:

When you're ready to clean up after yourself, avoid putting your pots and dishes in the sink. You will end up with one monster of a plumbing bill. Instead, let the excess wax cool and store it in plastic bags or other containers separated by color and scent. Wash out your tools with hot water outside, or by wiping them with a paper towel that gets properly disposed of.

Specific Types of Candles

There are a lot of candles that you can learn to make. What I'm covering here are those that will be easy and quick and require the least amount of ingredients and fussing.

Rolling, Rolling, Rolling

For time-challenged readers, the fastest candle by far is a rolled candle. For this you'll need wax rolling sheets in the color desired, any herbs or oils you want, a pair of scissors, and wick. Begin by cutting a square or rectangle whose length is the desired length of the candle. The width should be two times the length for nice burning time.

Warm the sheet of wax so it's pliable. One easy way is by placing it in the sunlight (this doesn't run up utility bills, and it spiritually charges the wax with solar energy). Next, lay the wick on the edge closest to you, with about 1 inch hanging out the top, and start rolling, making sure the candle is tight. If you're using oils, rub the inside of the wax with them. For powdered herbs, sprinkle these on evenly (note that you may have to gently heat the entire candle for a moment when you're done so the herbs stay firmly in place. This can be accomplished with a hair dryer).

A neat twist (literally) on the rolled candle begins by slicing a diagonal into the sheet wax from the upper left corner to the lower right corner. The long side is where you place your wick, and the rolling is the same, except that now the result will be a spiral, which is a fantastic magickal symbol. The spiral can represent cycles, reincarnation, protection, and transformation.

Another option is using sheet wax of varying colors. To accomplish this you will need to slice pieces of the sheet wax and warm the edges (again with a hair dryer) to join them. If need be, melt a little white wax and seal the slices on the inside of the sheet. Then roll as before, preferably as a spiral candle. The candle will have varying layers of color.

When you're done rolling the candle, get one of your melting pans out and heat it up. Put just the bottom of the rolled candle firmly on the bottom of the pan, allowing a little wax to melt. This seals the candle and ensures that you have a flat bottom.

Poured Candles

This is a very versatile approach to candle-making, and also very quick one. You can use all kinds of molds for poured candles, including wooden ones, glass (for self-contained candles) those for gelatin, natural molds (like sand, halved orange peels, and sea shells), and the venerable ice cube tray or milk carton mold, the latter of which is disposable.

In terms of safety, self-contained candles are fantastic. In this case you want to choose a wide-mouthed, strong, glass, ceramic, or metal container into which to pour the wax. Set up the wick in advance using a strand that's longer than the container, an aluminum foil base for the wick to weight it down, and a pencil to tie the wick to, which will keep it in the middle of the mold. You can pour a little warm wax in the bottom and let it cool to secure the wick in place.

Glass containers are ideal for multi-colored wax. They also reveal the level of the poured and melting wax much more easily. No matter the choice of containers, it helps to keep your container candles small (less than 6 inches). Otherwise the candles burn out easily.

If you're making the container candle in multiple colors, there's a really neat effect you can get, other than layers. Just before one layer of wax cools completely, poke a toothpick or other sharp item into it at various points around the edge of the glass. Let this layer finish cooling, then pour the next one. This will give a drip or stripe effect where it can be seen. Or, you can add a layer of crushed ice or chunk wax to the process. This will give the finished piece a mottled appearance.

About the only difference between the molded candle and the self-contained is that the first will be taken out of the container in which it was created. You can certainly buy commercial molds, but the crafty kitchen witch will revel in finding ones readily available around the house. In particular, I love the ice cube tray's pop-out candle action! I use these for spells to disperse anger or cool a heated situation because the symbolic value of an ice cube's imagery carries over nicely into the sacred space.

The only thing you have to be careful of is making sure you lightly oil the inside of your mold. After the wax solidifies, try to remove the candle. If it doesn't slide out, run a little hot water over the outside of the mold and try again. By the way, even if you discover a mold hasn't worked quite as you hoped, you can always re-melt the wax and try again.

Special Project 1: Flower Power

Take a small balloon and fill the bottom with some cool water (the amount depends on how large you want your wax flower to be). Melt waxes of different colors in separate pots, adding aroma as desired. When the wax reaches about 150 degrees, dip the balloon in the wax 3/4 of the way up. Repeat after one minute in a second, third, or fourth color until the wax is a 1/4-inch thick. Place the waxed balloon on a flat surface briefly, then let it cool. Pop the balloon and carve the remaining shell into the shape of petals, filling the center with magickally empowered potpourri.

I also enjoy making sand candles. To do this yourself, the sand needs to be damp and compact. This way you can shape it (and the dampness also affords some protection from burns and wax fires). Do not pour hot wax directly into the sand, as this will tend to disrupt the shape you've made. Instead pour it onto a spoon that slowly empties evenly onto the sandy surface. This needs to cool for about four hours. Then use a hair dryer to melt the exterior sand on the candle into the wax so it doesn't fall off easily.

Decorating Tips

Once you've finished making a candle, it's not that difficult to add nuances to it. For example, say you'd like to add a

Special Project 2: Winter Snow Candles

This technique is fantastic for making wax look like snow, whipped cream, cotton, and other fluffy things. For the magickal practitioner, it offers a wonderful opportunity to make Winter or Yule candles whose appearance honors the season.

To begin, take 1/2 pound of paraffin and heat it to 160 degrees. Add 1/2 tbs. cornstarch and beat with a hand beater. As you do, the wax will begin taking on the appearance of whipped cream. Shape this around a central red or white candle (or just shape it any way you wish around a pre-set wick). As the wax cools, sprinkle some silver or gold glitter on top so it shimmers in its own light.

magickal emblem. Wrap the candle with masking tape, leaving only the pattern of the emblem uncovered. Do this carefully, as you will be re-dipping the candle in another color so that the emblem stands out from the other wax. For the greatest amount of success with this technique, leave the original candle in a warm location while you heat the new wax to about 145 degrees. Dip it once or twice to achieve the desired effect, then put it immediately into cold water to get a shiny finish.

Another lovely touch that many magickal people seem to like is that of adding herbs and flowers to a finished candle. To accomplish this, simply dip the desired item in melted wax. Warning: the wax shouldn't be too hot. Just past the melting point will do. Note that you may have to gently move or shape flowers so they lay flat, but the wax usually prevents breakage. Immediately place the item where you wish on the candle. Continue on all sides of the candle until you're done, then dip the entire finished piece in a clear wax. As before, putting the candle immediately into a cold bath will keep the exterior shiny.

A third decorating method requires some stencils, a small paint brush, and candle bits and pieces of whatever color is desired. Lay the stencil on the finished candle you wish to decorate. Melt the candle wax bits and let them cool until 1/8 inch on top is translucent. Dip your paint brush into the wax, and apply it to the stencil. Remove the stencil very carefully to avoid blurring.

For those of you who like carving wands or staves, the fourth decorating method will give you a new medium in which to try your skill. In this case, warm your carving tools and create whatever patterns you wish in the wax. Some find it easier to draw a pattern first in pencil, and then carve. This particular method is doubly beautiful if you dip the candle in various layers of wax, each of which bears a different hue. Then the carving reveals the layering.

Problems and Solutions

It's inevitable that you will encounter periodic problems in candle-making until you get the knack of it. This list will help you know what may have gone wrong and how to fix it.

It's very important that you be patient with yourself in this (or any) art. No one becomes an expert overnight, and frustration isn't the kind of energy you want filling your magickal candles. When you find you're not being successful, take a break and try again later. You can always use a prefabricated candle for your spells and rituals in the interim.

Problem:	Solution:
Bubbles	Slow down the rate at which you pour wax into the mold.
Cracks	This happens usually when a candle cools too quickly. Don't rush the process.
Dulled surface	This is perfectly normal. Candles shine up nicely by polishing with a very soft cloth.
Faded color	Keep candles out of sunlight when not in use.
Hole in the middle	Pour more wax into that area as the candle is cooling.
Layer separation	This happens when wax is added too cold. If more than 1/8 inch has solidified, it's too cold.
Mixed layers	Either you didn't let the initial layer cool enough, or you poured the second one when the wax was too hot.
Mottled appearance	Increase the temperature of the mold before pouring wax in. You can do this by putting it in the microwave or oven for a few minutes. Alternatively, you may have used too much oil inside.
Odd color	You may have accidentally used a pan or utensil with another color wax on it, or gotten some dirty wax. If the later, wax can be re-melted and filtered through cheese cloth.
Stuck in the mold	Use more oil and be careful when adding more wax not to disrupt the smooth connection between the original wax and the container wall.

Magickal Candlecraft

Adding the spiritual dimension to candle-making really isn't overly difficult, it's just different. For one thing, rather than just thinking about the process itself, you will need to hold your specific magickal goal in mind while you work. This infuses the candle with a specific energy that matches your goal. Then, when the candle ignites, it begins releasing that energy. Sound simple? It is, and that's the beauty of it!

But this is just one of several ways in which you can saturate candles with the best possible vibrations. Other methods that will support your goals include:

1. Choosing a color that somehow mirrors your need or goal (refer to the chart provided in both the spellcraft and ritual sections for ideas).

2. Shaping the candle so that the final configuration represents your goal in manifested form. If you're not overly artistic or don't have access to molds, simple geometrics are an excellent option. Specifically:

    ᔓ Circle: Cycles, completion, protection, sacred space, the sun or the moon (color can   determine this), family/tribe, wholeness, equality, spellcraft, fate.

    ᔓ Cross: Discovery, finding items, decision- making, elemental balance, family ties (spiritual).

    ᔓ Square: Foundations, Earth magick, grounding, conscious mind, learning, physical health, truth, trust.

    ᔓ Triangle: Body-mind-spirit connection, fertility, life's energy, fulfillment, sexuality (especially for women).

    If making a shape proves difficult, carve an image into the candle instead.

3. Adding to the candle mix herbs, flowers, and oils that are also indicative of the candle's purpose. Some examples of this are provided in Chapter 5, and more correspondences follow here:

ᔆ Almond: Divination, healing, spellcraft, discernment.

ᔆ Allspice: Luck, inventiveness.

ᔆ Anise: Youthful energy and outlooks, banishing bad dreams, protection.

ᔆ Apple: Beauty, divination, fruitfulness, health.

ᔆ Banana: Offerings, fertility, abundance, male sexuality.

ᔆ Basil: Devotion, love, happiness.

ᔆ Bay: Victory, love, future-telling, wishes.

ᔆ Cedar: Abundance, safety, cleansing, psychism.

ᔆ Chamomile: Earth magick, victory, decreasing anxiety.

ᔆ Cinnamon: Dcsire, intuition, cleansing, energy.

ᔆ Daisy: Divination, joy, youthful outlooks, wish fulfillment.

ᔆ Ginger: Power, warm emotions, communication skills.

ᔆ Heather: Fate and fortune, glamoury, beauty, ghosts.

ᔆ Lavender: Glamoury, harmony, cleansing, peacefulness, manifesting magick.

ᔆ Lemon: Cleansing, devotion, poppet magick, positive emotions.

ᔆ Marjoram: Turning negativity, mental awareness, joy, safety.

- Mint: Decreasing stress, hospitality, focus, hope, joy, education, spirituality.

- Nutmeg: Alertness, understanding, education, memory.

- Orange: Devotion, fidelity, lifting tension, joy.

- Peach: Fortune-telling, abundance, wisdom, honesty, prosperity.

- Pine: Cleansing, turning away negativity, healing, success.

- Rose: Love (all kinds), spirituality, fairy magick, promises, meditation, karma.

- Rosemary: Improving the conscious mind.

- Sage: Banishing, cleansing, wisdom, wishes, dream magick.

- Thyme: Fairy magick, courage, dream work, cleansing, vitality.

- Vanilla: Joy, friendship, love, desire.

- Violet: Devotion, forgiveness, trust, rest.

4. Sizing the candle so it suits the magickal application. For example, you'll want a large candle for something that represents a long-term goal. Small candles can represent immediate needs, and they work nicely for everyday spells.

5. Stirring the candle's components clockwise to attract positive energy or counterclockwise to turn away unwanted influences.

6. Adding crystals to the base of the candle (or as part of its external decoration) that further promote the magick. Note that with metals, an alternative option is putting the candle in that type of holder.

Here's a brief chart of stone, crystal, and metal correspondences to which you can refer:

- ✎ Agate: Dream work, communication, prosperity, harmony wishes, safety, banishing fear.
- ✎ Amber: Glamoury, bravery, profuseness, victory, physical prowess.
- ✎ Amethyst: Protection, beauty, learning, devotion, spiritual focus, intuition, inner peace.
- ✎ Beryl: Hospitality, friendship, legal matters, education incitement.
- ✎ Bloodstone: Openings, prophetic ability, power, honesty, communication.
- ✎ Brass: Financial prosperity, sun magick, health.
- ✎ Copper: Healing, spirit communication, mental keenness.
- ✎ Coral: Water magick, focus, dream work, long life, peaceful sleep, protecting children
- ✎ Iron: Foundations, strength, turning negative energy, avoiding mischievous fairies.
- ✎ Jade: Earth magick, fortune, prayerfulness, rain magick.
- ✎ Lead: Grounding, safety, spellcraft, working with spirits, future-telling.
- ✎ Lodestone: Attracting energies to you, sexual prowess, fidelity, accord.
- ✎ Moonstone: Lunar magick, insight, psychism, gardening.
- ✎ Obsidian: Foundations, grounding unwanted energy.
- ✎ Onyx: Symmetry, desire, safety.

- Quartz: All-purpose energy booster, clarity, divinatory candles, vision.

- Seashells: Water magick, cycles, divinatory efforts, change.

- Silver: The moon, the Goddess, intuitive senses.

- Tin: Good fortune, travel magick.

- Turquoise: Protection, safety, success, turning fear.

Even if you don't have a New Age store in your area, you may be able to find tumbled crystals at nature and science shops, and on the Internet at sites like *www.e-witch.com.*

7. Making the candle at significant times. Every hour of the day, every phase of the moon, and many stellar configurations have specific metaphysical meanings that the savvy candle maker can tap for more power (think like a cosmic Tim Allen!). Use this list as a starting point if you're not familiar with common astrological associations:

- Dark Moon: Banishing, rest, sleep, turning negativity, introspection and meditation.

- New Moon (first sliver): New beginnings, changing cycles.

- Waxing Moon: Steady growth, positive transformation, attracting specific energies to you.

- Full Moon: Maturity, wisdom, insight, fertility, dreamwork, magickal mysteries, power, Goddess.

- Waning Moon: Decrease, releasing, letting go of the past.

- Blue Moon: Miracles and unexpected blessings.

> Dawn: Beginnings, hope, youthfulness, rebirth, refreshed outlooks.

> Noon: God energy, Fire magick, strength, leadership, truth, conscious mind.

> Dusk: Endings and closure.

> Midnight: The witching hour, good for all types of magick.

If you'd like more information on how sun signs and moon signs affect magick, I recommend buying a good astrological calendar every year.

8. Adding something personal to the blend. Traditional additions from magickal history include spit, hair, fingernails, blood, and semen. Why such odd things? Because the ancients believed that blood, for example, bore an imprint of the person through whom it ran. By using something so personal, they were marking that candle for personal use, similar to animals marking territory using urine. I realize this sounds extreme, and I would only advocate this for a candle you plan to use for yourself, but there is a very strong historical precedence for it.

9. Carving the candle with runes, symbols, initials, or other images that have personal meaning.

10. Using symbolic candle holders. Thankfully the New Age market provides us with a huge variety of creative candle holders, some of which match magickal goals very nicely (like heart-shaped taper holders for love spells).

   Bear in mind that you don't have to add *all* these dimensions to get positive results. The most important factor is your willful focus and making each step of the process personally meaningful. Beyond those basics, everything else is the proverbial icing on the cake.

Applied Candle Magick

If you must purchase candles rather than making them yourself, then applied candle magick should include a couple of extra steps. The first is cleansing the candle. After all, it's been lying around the store for who knows how long, picking up random energy that could prove detrimental to your work.

There are three good ways to rid a candle of unwanted energy. One is to simply rub it with a little wine or other type of alcohol while focusing on your goal. Begin at the top and move downward, so the energy moves toward the earth, where it can be reabsorbed. No need to leave negative vibes lying around! The second method is to move the candle through the smoke produced by a common cleansing incense like sage, and the third is to sprinkle it with a bit of salt water or lemon water.

Once this is completed, you can dedicate your candle for a purpose. Handmade candles have been dedicated throughout the creation process just by the materials chosen and the person's focus. Mass-produced candles may have a latent use built in by color or shape, but you still need to "set" the magical purpose into the wax. To accomplish this you can carve an image of the goal in the candle and dab that image with a bit of your skin oil (this marks the candle as yours).

Alternatively you can bless the candle by calling on a personal god or goddess to saturate the candle with it's purpose. By the way, once you have designated a candle for a specific use, make sure you store it with an appropriate label! It makes things much easier when you're looking for spell and ritual components.

With both cleansing and consecration out of the way, you can now think about anointing your candle. This is a way to add an aromatic dimension to the magick, and of course it also has symbolic value. Just remember that the general rule of thumb is to rub oil onto the candle from the bottom up for attracting specific energies, or from the top down to banish or expel. You are now ready to start making magick!

And just how can candles be applied in magick? The ways are as varied as your imagination. Candles can represent needs and goals, they can become poppets, they can simply create a warm ambiance for your ritual work, and they can even symbolize the Divine. But rather than just talking about using candles, let's go ahead and try various processes so you can see which techniques you like best.

Salamander Scrying

Secrets are revealed by the subtle spirit of fire.
—Nostradamus

W hy was a candle's flame so special to early people? Above and beyond affording precious light in which to accomplish tasks the day would not otherwise allow, world mythology often depicts fire as an element stolen from the gods themselves. It stands to reason that if the gods held fire as a "secret," then it must be a very magickal thing, indeed!

Although modern folk don't necessarily think the same way about fire as our ancestors did, there is no denying the enchanting power of a candle's flame. It seems to smile and wave at anyone who will look. Some call the spirit of the flame a salamander, and it is said that it lives only as long as the fire. If one should ask the spirit a question, it will sometimes answer by its movements and shape. As we observe the salamander's dance, our eyes and spirits are captured, and we begin to enter different levels of seeing and being than those achieved by day-to-day living.

Thus we come to the ancient art of scrying by fire. To scry means to view distantly or view carefully. This is actually the root word for the modern term "discern," which describes scrying very well. The idea is to teach yourself a new way of seeing and perceiving, and by so doing receive messages and insights from a divinatory tool, in this case a simple candle.

Helpful Hints

Use this guideline when preparing for candle divination:

- ℘ Choose the candle's color so it matches the theme of your question, like green for money or red for matters of the heart. The color considered generically good for any divination effort is pale yellow.

- ℘ Dab the candle with a bit of sympathetic oil to improve the specificity of the results. Sticking with the previous example, patchouli is good for money matters, and rose is good for love. Alternatively you can dab the candle with a bit of your personal cologne or perfume if the question is a personal one.

- ℘ Work where there is no wind to disrupt the results.

- ℘ Work in a fire-safe area, using sturdy candle holders (also see Chapter 8).

- ℘ Work where you won't be interrupted. Turn off the television and telephone, and find a private space. Concentration is essential to any divinatory effort.

- ℘ Work only when you're well-rested and in a positive frame of mind. Anger, sadness, sickness, and other negative situations can adversely skew the results of your efforts.

ॐ Consider setting up a sacred space for your efforts. This will keep unwanted energy influences from affecting the result. For those of you who are unsure about how to create sacred space, an example of casting follows here:

Sample Circle Casting for Candle Divination

Take a blessed, anointed white candle and light it while standing in the center of the area where you will be doing the divination. Visualize a circle of silver-white surrounding the candle's flame, and move to the eastern part of that circle. Stop and say, "As the sun crosses the windy horizon bringing the dawn of a new day, so do I hold a candle in the darkness. May it awaken my senses."

Next, move to the South of the same circle. Visualize the silvery candlelight remaining in the air behind you so that the first part of the circle shimmers with its glow. When you reach the South say, "The noonday sun chases the shadows and grants understanding. So let this candle bring me true sight."

Continue on to the West, keeping the visualization in mind as you walk. Now over half the circle burns with the candle's energy in your mind's eye. Stop when you reach the western point and say, "The sun goes down and kisses the sea with gentle warmth, so too let this candle warm my heart and spirit."

Move again to the North as before, imagining the candlelight circle surrounding all but this last point. Say, "Even in the Earth's darkness, there is light and hope. Lift the veils between the worlds that I may look beyond and find answers. So be it."

Now go sit in front of the candle and begin. When you finish with the divinatory effort it is nice to reverse the process by walking counterclockwise and blowing out the candle when you reach East. If you wish, thank the elements and sacred powers for protecting you and offering insights (a thankful heart is one far more open to receiving revelations again in the future).

✎ Consider meditating beforehand to settle your mind and spirit. For those who have never tried meditating, don't feel you have to look like a pretzel for the effort to be successful. Just sit down where you'll be comfortable and follow this basic guideline:

Meditation to Prepare for Candle Divination

Put on some quiet music and light the candle you plan to use. Look at the candle for a moment so you can see it clearly in your mind's eye without seeing it, then close your eyes. Breathe deeply and evenly. Release the tensions and mundane thoughts from the day and turn your thoughts to the image of the candle. Don't think about the specifics, just the light, glow, and warmth that surrounds it. Reach out to that welcoming light and embrace it. Take it into yourself and hold it in your heart to provide energy and focus. Let it melt away any residual anxiety or uncertainty and think only of your question. When you feel as if that question has filled every fiber of your being (like the candlelight did), open your eyes and begin.

✎ Wash your hands before you begin to clean away any excess vibrations that linger from normal daily activity. A little salt water or lemon water is a good choice. An alternative is taking a bath so your entire aura is purified. Put a little lavender in a piece of secured cloth, along with ginger and sage for peace, energy, and purification, respectively.

✎ Keep your mind on the question throughout the process, waiting until that process is completed to ponder potential interpretations.

✎ Interpret the symbols and signs by measuring them against your heart and personal meaning first, then turn to the key provided here or in other symbol collections for alternative and/or more detailed insights.

৯ Make notes of the results you get for future reference. This is very important, as you will find symbolic themes repeat themselves over time, which in turn makes future interpretations much easier. Additionally, some readings won't make sense for a while. Return to those that seem enigmatic in a week, a month, or a year, and read them over. Insights will come when the time is right.

By the way, you need not use all these ideas every time you undertake a divinatory effort. What's most important is that the steps you take are meaningful and put you in the right frame of mind for the task at hand.

Types of Candle Divination

Historically speaking there were many ways of performing candle divination and even more ways of interpreting the results from those visionary excursions. What I'm presenting here are the methods that don't need a lot of extra components, that are easy to learn, and that usually don't require hours and hours of free time to achieve some level of success.

Pyromancy

This is the most traditional and common form of candle divination. Set up a candle in an area where it will be at a comfortable eye level in a sturdy, safe container (no need to set the house on fire!). Make yourself comfortable—it's hard to scry if you feel cramped or awkward.

Next, whisper your question to the candle and light it. Sit down and loosen up your muscles (if you're wearing your shoulders in your ears this won't work). Close your eyes for a minute. Leave everything other than you, the candle, and the question out of the mental space you're presently occupying.

When you feel centered, look toward the candle, but not directly at it. Let your eyesight blur a bit, and take deep, even breaths. Now simply observe what the candle does while you're thinking of your question. Here is a list of potential interpretive values for your consideration:

- Active, bright burning: A positive, "yes" answer.
- Blazing suddenly: Something unexpected headed your way.
- Blue flame (predominant color): A lack of energy impedes progress. This can also indicate the presence of a ghost.
- Candle won't light: A huge stop sign. Something's wrong and you need to rethink things before proceeding.
- Faint burning: This indicates similar faint-heartedness regarding the question. You are obviously uncertain and it might be best to hold off on this decision or action until other matters reconcile themselves.
- Flickering: A lack of energy to support this decision or action. Build yourself up, then act. Otherwise you won't get the results you hope for.
- Halo: Be cautious. Trouble is on the way.
- Long-burning, bright flame: Good fortune.
- Movement in the flame: Things are changing and transforming. If the flame moves predominantly to the left, the changes may not be good.
- Orange flame (predominant color): Warm feelings and pleasurable times.
- Red flame (predominant color): Don't let anger and emotions rule your actions.
- Rings in the flame: Good news. Happiness.
- Smoldering: Trouble is brewing. Hold on tight.

- ❧ Split flame: Two equally appealing options make themselves known.
- ❧ Three-tip flame: Take the middle road, where you can find balance.
- ❧ Wax dripping: On the left side a negative sign, on the right a positive one. In a spiral it indicates the presence of a spirit who may have a message for you.
- ❧ Yellow flame (predominant color): Get creative and communicate!

I should note at this juncture that some people find they actually see symbolic or literal pictures in the flame. If this happens to you, don't shut down. Go with it! The fire light may have helped you achieve a trance-like state that's more open to receiving imagery from the Higher Self and the Sacred. Or it may be that you are simply more attuned to the energy of fire than most people.

For those of you who find the candle doesn't seem to react in any unusual manner, try bringing it closer to you and starting again. Sometimes our aura communicates more effectively with the flame than our mind or will. Another alternative is observing the candle's flame via a reflective surface like a mirror or dark bowl filled with water. Because each person's eyesight differs, observing the flame in different media may resolve your problems. Should these suggestions prove unsuccessful, don't despair. This can happen for any number of reasons, including:

- ❧ Loss of concentration during the process.
- ❧ Interruptions (external noise included).
- ❧ Compromised mental or physical state (weariness, sickness, anger, and so on don't usually produce good divination sessions).

Besides these three, there are simply times when fate's web is too tangled to tell you anything definitive. Wait a few days or weeks and try again, or try another candle divination method. If the car doesn't work, change vehicles!

Ceromancy

Ceromancy is divination by the patterns produced in wax and was very common in Mexico and Spain. To practice it, rather than placing the candle in a holder, you grasp it as it burns and think of a question. Tilt the candle over a surface that won't be damaged by the wax (paper or water are two good choices), while continuing to focus on that question.

The results of this activity may be interpreted similarly to ink blots or tea leaves. Specifically, a heart close to you might represent a relationship blossoming, or someone you love returning home. A number could represent the number of days, weeks, or months, before the question at hand resolves itself. Initials might pertain to important people in the question, and so forth. Here are a few other common symbols that show up:

- Anchor: Foundations, also something holding you back.
- Apple: Pay attention to your mental or physical health.
- Arrow: Messages, often about a relationship.
- Ant: Tenacity is the key to success.
- Bell: News, alternatively the need for protection.
- Book: Abstract ideas, study.
- Broom: Time for some spiritual housecleaning.
- Bubbles: Hopes; if the bubbles break, the hope will not be fulfilled.
- Butterfly: Transformation, alternatively vanity.
- Cauldron: Ancient symbol of the Goddess. Reconnect with her.

- Circle: Cycles, the moon (or sun), protection.
- Coin: Money. If there are several, finances may soon improve.
- Cross: Decisions. A crossroad.
- Crystal: The need for clarity.
- Door: An opening or closing.
- Dragonfly: Good luck heading your way.
- Eye: Insight. Are you looking at things correctly?
- Feather: Lighten up—you're being too serious.
- Finger: Accusations that may or may not be deserved.
- Flame: A hot situation. Be careful.
- Hand: You may need help, or perhaps offer it to another.
- Heart: Emotional matters (look at the heart's shape for more insight).
- Ice cube: A chilly reception.
- Key: A chance to unlock a mystery.
- Light bulb: Ideas in the making. Creativity.
- Lightning bolt: A flash of awareness, sometimes painful.
- Maze or labyrinth: A sacred journey.
- Mouth: Are you speaking what's truly in your heart?
- Pen: Effective communication is necessary.
- Pentagram: Magick awakens!
- Pillar: Lean on others for support now.
- Ring: An engagement or marriage. Alternatively, other types of promises and commitments (like business partnerships) in the making.
- Scroll: Karmic law unfolding.

- Shoe: The need to walk away or toward a situation.
- Square: Earth or elemental matters. Foundations.
- Star: A secret wish.
- Teardrops: Temporary sadness.
- Triangle: Fate. The three-fold nature brought into balance.
- Tree: Growth, strength, life.
- Umbrella: Inclement weather (often emotional).
- Vines: Someone is being very clingy.
- Web: The need to network and connect.
- X: The treasure you seek is right under your nose.
- Y: A yes answer or an initial.

By the way, don't limit your imagination in terms of what type of pattern the wax has made. Some people see runes in the wax, others see whole three-dimensional pictures! Go with your first gut instinct and ask yourself what that image means to you personally. If you can't think of any specific interpretive value, then look that imagery up in a dream guide or other similar symbol dictionary. Also, I've found that using several colors of wax sometimes improves the symbolic results of this effort. So if you're having trouble finding any patterns or imagery with one candle, try using two or three and see if it provides better sensual cues.

Causimomancy

Causimomancy is divination by burning items in a sacred fire, including the fire produced by a blessed candle. For example, in Europe people would burn a dry mistletoe leaf in a candle flame. If it sparked, it meant anger was holding the querist back, whereas a steady flame indicated devotion and good motivations. Similarly, it is said that if one burns a pea with a candle flame, and it flares up, it's a good omen.

In modern magick the most popular thing to burn is paper, usually with the question or symbols written upon it. The burning here does two things: It provides a second flame whose movements and behavior are observed for omens, and it releases your questions to the universe by way of the smoke produced (by the way, divining by the smoke produced is technically called capnomancy).

To try this yourself, you will need not only a candle but a good, fire-safe container. One option is a stoneware bowl filled with sand or dirt. This is where you'll place the burning item to observe it. Then:

- Choose an item to burn. It can be a flower petal, herb, piece of cotton string, paper, or any other natural material that somehow represents your question. Please make sure this item is not one to which you might have an allergic reaction when it smokes.
- If using paper, write your question literally or symbolically on it (this can also be dabbed with a hint of oil if you wish).
- Hold the chosen item in hand and focus on your question, pouring the energy of your will into it.
- Reach out toward the candle and ignite the item along one edge carefully.
- As soon as it's burning evenly, put it into the fire-safe container and watch what happens.

The results of this activity can be interpreted in much the same manner as the pyromantic symbols provided earlier in this chapter. Additionally, if the item:

- Burns completely and quickly, this is a good sign. It may also indicate a desire that manifests far sooner than expected.

ᕱ Burns only part way, this is a 50-50 proposition and you may want to reconsider your options.

ᕱ Smolders and goes out, the answer is no.

ᕱ Burns noisily, the answer is yes.

ᕱ Burns silently, beware of hidden matters.

ᕱ Doesn't ignite, a definitive no accompanied by a warning not to proceed further.

Tra The-Bon

A rather unique use for candle wax comes to us from Tibet. Here, and in certain parts of Arabia, the nail of a thumb is painted with red wax, then scried by the light of a single lamp (likely an oil or butter lamp). The thumb was not always that of the diviner's, however, but often that of a child, because children represent innocence and purity.

This method provides the modern practitioner with a lot of flexibility. One could, for example, dip a bay leaf into wax and scry the surface if you were asking about a creativity issue (bay is sacred to Apollo, a god who presides over inventiveness). Or you could paint a little red wax on a coffee cup to divine about why you're lacking energy (coffee represents energy, as does the color red). Another option is to follow the pattern provided by our ancestors and paint your own fingernail with a symbolic colored wax when asking about personal matters. In all cases, however, do be careful with the temperature of the wax. If it's too hot, you won't get a smooth scrying surface and could burn yourself.

If you are interested in learning about other types of divination, see my book *Futuretelling* (Crossing Press), which is an encyclopedia of divination methods and meanings.

Candles in Dreams

I would be remiss if I overlooked the powerful symbolism of candles in other settings besides those mentioned in this chapter. Even with the advent of modern lighting, they often appear in our dreams as representations, omens, and signs for our consideration. If a candle appears in your dreams, here are some of the ways it can be interpreted according to various dream keys:

- An awakening; enlightenment.
- The birth of an idea, insight, imagination, or spiritual awareness.
- The human spirit or soul.
- Birth, life, or death (depending on whether it's unlit, lit, or blown out, respectively).
- Hope.
- Guidance (light in the darkness).
- Devotion and constancy if the flame is clear and calm.

Bear in mind that dream interpretation is highly subjective, and there are a lot of other factors in a dream that may have meaning. For more information about dream imagery, you may wish to read my book *The Language of Dreams* (Crossing Press). This and *Futuretelling* are readily available online at *www.amazon.com*.

Candlelight 3 Spells and Charms

There are two ways of spreading light, to be the
candle or the mirror that reflects it.
—Edith Wharton

I would take Edith Wharton's idea one step further to say that a third way of spreading light is using the energy of a candle for magick. Throughout the world's history, candles have taken part in spells, charms, amulets, talismans, and fetishes. Although the exact role changes from era to era and region to region, the light of the candle reaches out from this history and calls to us to follow. Why? There is something in the human psychological makeup that responds to candlelight in positive spiritual ways. Additionally, anything that's been used so consistently for magickal purposes develops an inherent communal power that supports and sustains our efforts.

Candles in Spellcraft

Thankfully, candlelight spells have not fallen out of fashion, nor has the legacy been lost. Our modern practices still have components that reach back to the earliest forms of candle magick and link us to our spiritual roots. Better still, candle spellcraft is still considered a staple to folk magicians around the world. To get things rolling, let's first look at the common elements of candlelight spells. By mixing and matching these elements into a meaningful combination, one can easily create spells for any occasion or need.

Element 1: Color Symbolism

The choice of a candle's color when it's being used for spellcraft is important, as it represents the person or matter at hand. Typically the symbolic values follow this chart (with minor personal variations or those that come from a specific cultural or familial tradition):

Color Chart for Spellcraft Candles

The symbolism for colored candles in rituals (Chapter 5) can easily be applied to spellcraft and charms. However, you'll find this list far more extensive, and useful for nearly any type of magick that you plan to undertake. As always, please use this as a starting point, not an edict. If a color has different meaning for you, always go with that instinct first.

Black: Banishing, closure, Earth magick, true-seeing, turning negativity, death.

Brown: Grounding, foundations, Earth magick, security, confidence, the conscious mind, tenacity.

Gold: Masculine energy, Fire magick, mental power, developing personal talents and skills, victory, luck, originality.

Green: Money, growth and maturity, abundance, Earth magick, fortune and fate, green magick, revitalization, health.

Midnight Blue: Water, instinct, innovation, dream magick, transformation, devotion, contemplation, magick.

Orange: Energy (less potent than red), motivation, nurturing, smooth adjustments, attracting positive energy.

Pink: Friendship, gentle love, goddess energy, emotions, unity, health, revival.

Purple: Leadership, authority, composure, spiritual matters, mediumship, magick, augmenting psychic awareness, sound spiritual judgement.

Red: Vitality, energy, life's blood, sexuality, bravery, zeal, will, overcoming, victory, protection from fairies.

Silver: Feminine energy (the goddess), the moon, protection, occult awareness and magickal energy, imagination.

Sky blue: Forbearance, endurance, joy, psychism, beginnings, awareness, comprehension, travel magick, accord.

Violet: Finding things, adeptness, advancement or progress, inspiration, dream work, karmic understanding, balance, divination.

White: Protection, cleansing, the moon, purity, truthfulness, harmony, focus, meditative clarity. White is the all-purpose color when other candles aren't available.

Yellow: The mind, inventiveness, knowledge, self-assurance, charm and glamoury spells, communication (all forms), divination.

The degree of a color is also an important consideration to bear in mind. The deeper a color is, the more powerful the result tends to be. Additionally, the symbolic value may change a bit. Dark blue is good for inner harmony and light blue seems good as a meditative color that inspires mental peace. Similarly, if a candle is a combination of two colors (as peach is a combination of orange and pink), *both* colors affect the overall energy of that candle and it's final application. For example, peach might be used to nurture a friendship.

Element 2: Carving or Shaping

In spell books or collections of magickal methods it's quite common to find instructions on carving an image into a candle, or using a candle of a specific shape (which you can buy that way, make that way, or carve that way). In love spells, for example, it's common to use a sharp point, like that of a toothpick or pin, to carve a heart into the candle wax. The image of a heart is so strongly associated with emotions, specifically love, that most people have little trouble using this approach. The key to success, however, is that the person doing the carving and casting the spell equates the heart with love and can really put some willpower into that focus.

A rather gruesome illustration of shaping comes from ancient Europe (predominantly Scotland and Ireland). There, candles were sometimes formed from the fat of a hanged person to look like a hand (or attached to the preserved hand itself). A thief would burn this as he entered a house to make the residents stay asleep while their possessions were neatly taken away.

A second illustration of shaping is the person-shaped candles sometimes used in Voodoo and related traditions. In this instance, the candle wax is sometimes mixed with other components to improve the sympathetic value of the candle with the person it represents. The candle may not always be burned, it may act as a poppet. For example, if one were to use such a candle to extend protective energy to another, the candle's wax might be mixed with protective herbs like frankincense and myrrh and then formed into the shape of a person. Next, the candle might be wrapped in cloth and put in a padded box, or other similar measures might be taken. In effect, this surrounds the intended person with similar safety.

In applying this basic concept for modern magick, whatever shape one creates must also create a deep emotional attachment or response. This principle is the core of sympathetic magick. For example, when shaping a candle so it bears the form of a pregnant woman in order to help with fertility, you must have tremendous love for this image of self and the child growing in it's belly, even though it's only a symbolic representation. In magick a symbol is just as potent as what it represents. You must also be able to direct that love to yourself. Love has tremendous manifesting power.

So, no matter which elements here you choose, this basic guideline still applies: If it's not meaningful, if it doesn't evoke strong emotions and connections, don't waste your time. Find another candle spell or make one yourself that meets your needs, or the magick will not work.

Element 3: Dressing and Adorning

To dress a candle typically means to dab it with an aromatic oil whose scent matches the goal of a spell. An alternative is to rub the candle with skin oil or personal perfume. As with carving, it's very important to focus on your intention while dressing the candle. In effect, you are carving your will into the candle through the oil.

Adorning is similar to dressing but more literal. For example, a candle being used for a binding spell might get bound in white thread or cloth and never lit. Instead, this candle gets put away, even as one wishes the person or situation to stay away. Other ways of adorning a candle include:

- ೭ Attaching a piece of your hair to it (this marks the candle with personal energy and intention).
- ೭ Binding a small swatch of cloth to it. This typically belongs to the person to whom the energy is being directed. Put the swatch way at the bottom of the candle for safety reasons.

֍ Pressing a tiny crystal into the base or center of the candle. Placement at the base represents supportive energy, and placement in the middle represents a focus point, meaning the crystal represents the spell's goal.

֍ Surrounding the candle with supportive herbs or elemental items. For example, a spell focused on emotional healing might employ a floating candle (a candle surrounded by water), because water has a natural affinity for both healing and the emotional nature. A spell to keep one's feet on the ground might follow this methodology by including a brown candle based in dirt.

As you can see, dressing and adorning add extra symbolic dimensions to your spells, which in turn usually improve the results. The more sensual cues (visual, aromatic, and so on) you can provide your superconscious, the better you'll be able to direct your will and the magickal energy.

Element 4: Pinning

I cannot begin to tell you how many spells I've read that include instructions about placing a straight pin through the middle or top third of a candle's wax before starting the rest of the spell. One example comes to us from England, where it was used as a love spell. A young person would put a straight pin through the candle, chanting something like, "It is not this candle that I stick, but ___'s heart to prick, awake or asleep let the right man/woman my heart keep." This process was repeated several times down the candle, with the names of several potential mates. When the candle burned out completely it was believed the "right" person would come a-calling.

For our purposes, the pin is like an X marking the spot where magick will be released. Note, however, that as the candle burns down to this point, the practitioner needs to sustain his or her focus, effort, and will. If he or she does not, the results will either be lessened or nonexistent. After this procedure one may either save the candle remnant for another similar spell or ritually dispose of it by melting the wax.

Element 5: Timing

A lot of candle spells direct the practitioner to light the candle at a designated date or hour. I do not personally consider this an essential element, but it does have a lot of historical precedence. For the purposes of this book, I would suggest using timing elements if they (a) work with your schedule and (b) are meaningful to you.

Element 6: Silence

This is a very interesting element to candle spellcraft. Many older spells that I've read instruct the practitioner to remain silent for a certain amount of time before and/or after the spell is cast. There is a certain power to silence, not the least of which comes from giving yourself time to turn your mind away from mundane thoughts. By remaining quiet, you're not releasing energy. Instead, you internalize it, center yourself, and really focus. This advice is doubly worth heeding if the spell itself has a theme that supports silence—like stopping gossip.

Element 7: Lighting and Burning

As one might expect, most candle spells call for lighting the candle at a certain point in the magickal process, then burning the candle for a certain length of time. Let's look at each of these processes separately. First, lighting the candle quite literally sets the energy in motion. Think of the symbolic value alone, not to mention the natural energy of fire.

There are various points in a spell where a candle can be lit. One is at the outset of the working. This accomplishes several things. It can represent Spirit's part in your effort, it denotes an informal sacred space, it provides a focus, improves the ambience for magick, and represents your intention to do something metaphysical.

A second time is at the outset of, or during, an incantation. In magick, an incantation adds word power. It also brings the sense of hearing and a physical action (speaking) into the working to make it multi-dimensional. This in turn often improves the results. Here the candlelight represents the practitioner's will and goal, and the words of the incantation confirm that goal.

Finally, a candle might be lit at the end of the spell. This symbolizes the light of magick going out into the world and manifesting power. So when does the candle get blown out? That too depends on the spell.

Some spells instruct that the candle be allowed to burn completely out, thereby using all the energy placed therein for this one specific purpose. Other spells have the candle burn down to a specific level (like the placement of a pin, or a carving) before being extinguished. Others still advise blowing out the candle at a specific juncture in the spell (like after reciting the incantation) to release the energy. And other directions tell us to let the candle burn for a pre-set number of hours, the numeric value adding more symbolic energy.

Element 8: Chanting, Invoking, or Incantations

I spoke briefly earlier about word power for magick. Have you ever noticed how someone who speaks in negatives often has a life that's filled with negatives too? This is partly the result of the power of words. Sound has a very specific vibration that fills the areas in which we live and move. If those sounds are affirming, we see better results from our magick.

Chants are repeated phrases that improve personal focus, aid in achieving altered states, and have an almost musical quality. They can be done singly or in a group, but group chanting produces perhaps the greatest results because of a chant's ability to create a harmonious resonance among the members. It can also raise power.

An invocation is perhaps better called an invitation. This word power is designed to invite the presence of an elemental or other sacred power (like a god or goddess) into the area where the spell is being performed. This presence helps to empower, guide, and direct the energy from the spell. While we see this more frequently in a ritual context, it can certainly be part of spellcraft too.

The incantation is a phrase or set of phrases that detail the purpose of the spell. In some instances it also contains instructions for the spell. For example, if part of a spell's incantation says "by candlelight and ringing bell, I now release my magick spell," it makes sense to recite the word "candlelight" when igniting the candle, and recite "ringing bell" when ringing a little bell. Okay, I know, this brings up the question of why a bell would be used in a candle spell. The bell is another type of sound magick that carries the vibration of our spell outward from that spot, effectively announcing it to the four winds.

But what about moments when speaking out loud isn't possible (like when you are at work or another location ill-suited to magickal processes)? In this case, think your words inwardly. It has pretty much the same effect.

Element 9: Ritualistic overtones

Some people like to add minor ritualistic overtones to spellcraft. For example, when I do a spell for money, I give the universe some kind of offering. I might pour out wine, give something valuable to someone who needs it, or sell something that I cherish. Although this might sound odd, we are co-creators with the Sacred, which means doing our part to help with manifestation. By making a sacrifice or offering, you open the path for the universe to bless you threefold.

Another ritualistic addition is that of repeating a spell a set number of times, or over a certain length of time. In either instance, the number chosen has symbolic value that supports the spell's goal. Here is a brief list of numeric correspondences:

Number Correspondences

1—Unity, harmony, sun magick, teamwork, self.
2—Partnership, accord, balance.
3—The body-mind-spirit connection, tenacity, health.
4—Earth magick, foundations, structure, money.
5—Spiritual or psychic matters, adaptability, focus.
6—Devotion, thoroughness, protection.
7—Water and moon magick, well-being, foresight.
8—Leadership, self-control, power.
9—Truth, the threefold law, charity, legal matters.
10—Rational self, logic, conscious mind.

It should be noted that in terms of time, the number can equate to minutes, hours, days, weeks, months, and even years if a matter is serious enough to warrant on-going magickal support. Don't give up on your goals without giving the universe a reasonable amount of time to help you manifest them.

Element 10—Reusing Wax Remnants

This is a great way to recycle and increase the latent energy in your candles at the same time. Unless you're using dripless candles, it is highly likely that you will have bits and pieces of candles left from various magickal processes. If you keep these in little boxes or bags labeled according to the focus of the magick, you can then re-melt the remnants and let the leftover energy within mingle with other similar candles. Once the wax has cooled, you'll have the accumulated energy from several workings to support the next spell or ritual you undertake.

৩৩৩

As you can see, although candle magick is considered a "lesser" magick, in that it is a folk custom, it can become rather complex when you try to put all these options together. Don't let that dissuade you. Generally, it's best to choose a few personally significant elements that make sense considering the spell's goal, and keep it simple. If you're thinking so much about the process that it detracts your will and focus, all the extra bells and whistles won't matter!

Thematic Candle Spells

Before giving you some specific examples of candlelight spells to try or adapt, I'd like to mention that the candle is only a tool. There's nothing really special about that bit of wick and wax other than the willpower and focus you direct to it. So don't depend on a tool to accomplish anything metaphysically. You are the enabler; you are the magick.

That having been said, tools are helpful. Most of us haven't become wholly comfortable in our magickal skins yet—there is a part of us that says, "How can I possibly do something so amazing?" This is perfectly normal, and tools help us overcome that kind of difficulty by giving us something to focus on other than ourselves. This relieves a lot of the uncertainty that we would normally direct inward allowing us to attend to the task at hand. Eventually one would hope that all of us would become adept enough to forego the tools, but until then, here are some sample candle spells. I'm not including tons of them because the goal of this book is to help you create your *own* candle spells, charms, rituals, and so on. Nonetheless, like with sewing, it helps to have a pattern from which to cut the cloth. These examples represent good patterns that I have found successful. I hope you will too.

Attraction

This isn't a love spell in the traditional sense. Instead the idea is to simply extend "attractive" energy toward those who are best suited to being mates for you. Begin with a pink candle (a good color for warm feelings). Next, find a small magnet, like those used on refrigerators, and put it under the candle's base. This is for "magnetic" appeal. Focus on your goal to bring someone into your life (try not to focus on a specific person). Light the candle, saying something like:

> *To me, to me...come to me*
> *One who sees true with loving eyes*
> *One who is gentle and wise*
> *Come to me*
> *Like a magnet to metal, feel the pull of this spell*
> *Then trust your heart, and trust it well!*

Let the candle burn out naturally. If at all possible, maintain your focus while it burns to improve results. Afterward you can carry the magnet in a wallet or pocket as a charm (please don't do this if you work with computers regularly, however!).

Forgiveness/Peace

For this spell you will need to set a date and time with the person toward whom you wish to extend forgiveness so he or she can participate in the spell. Each person should bring a candle to represent the other individual. These get placed in the middle of a table (a middle ground) and lit. Each person then speaks honestly to the flame of his or her candle of his or her anger and pain. The candle flame represents the burning away of that negativity. Let the fire take your bad feelings. When both people have finished speaking their minds, they take each other's hands and say the following incantation (or a more personal one) three times:

> *What was spoken is now broken*
> *Bring us peace by the light of day*
> *Put our anger and sadness away.*

Blow out the candles and ritually bury or destroy them to symbolically put those feelings behind you. For this spell to be wholly effective, the situation that lead up to this should be regarded as dead and buried, not to be spoken of again without both people's consent.

Glamoury (Confidence)

Have you ever noticed how everything looks and feels different in candlelight? Well, the idea behind this spell is to bring that special energy into your aura and let it shimmer out to others. In this case you should buy or make a person-shaped candle in your favorite color. Put a small dab of personal perfume or cologne over the heart and forehead of the wax figure. If you wish, also adorn it with a swatch of cloth from a piece of your old clothing to create sympathy between you and the candle.

Next, light the candle and observe the glow of the flame. Notice how it too has an aura that extends beyond the fire. Visualize that light growing until it encompasses your entire body, then say:

> *I accept the light and this energy,*
> *To aid me in my glamoury!*
> *Within and without, shimmer and shine,*
> *So that confidence will be mine!*

Blow out the candle and carry the cloth swatch with you to keep the spell's energy close at hand for when you need to release a little of that confident demeanor.

Health

Take a green candle (a traditional healing hue) and carve your name in it. Dab a bit of camphor or thyme oil on the mid point of the candle, working it in both directions to achieve balance. As you do this say:

Good health be mine when e'er this candle shines!

Light the candle for a few minutes every day during your devotionals for ongoing wellness. Alternatively, light it for a longer time when you feel a cold or the flu coming on to give your body extra spiritual support with which to fight the bugs.

Joy

Take a sky blue candle, turn it upside down, and carve a frown (an upside down U) into the surface about mid-way down. If you wish, also press a small tumbled pink quartz or other personally preferred crystal into the wax just below the "face." Next, turn the candle upright to put it into its holder (this makes the frown look like a smile). Light the candle, saying:

"A smile is but a frown turned upside down!
Turn and change, turn and change
An attitude to rearrange!
Let joy be mine as this candle shines!

Light the candle when you say the word "shine," and let happiness replace the dark clouds in your spirit. The candle needs to burn down to the smile (but don't let the flame erase it). At this point you can remove the crystal and use it as a touchstone any time you feel depression setting in.

Karmic Fortune

This is a great spell that you can perform every day to increase the flow of luck, money, or other necessities in your life. Take a large glass bowl (like those for fish) and stand a simple white candle in the bottom of it. Every morning when you leave the house, or every night when you get home, light the candle and drop some coins in with a wish. When the bowl is completely filled, give this money to a friend in need or a charity, then replace the candle and start again. The good gesture will return to you threefold!

Psychic Awareness

This spell is a good adjunct to your candle divinations. Before attempting any psychic endeavor, take a yellow candle and carve the image of an eye into it. As you carve, chant quietly something like, "with eyes to true-see, let my vision be freed!" Light the candle and let it burn down to just above the eye. As it burns, use this time to meditate and focus on your question. When the flame reaches the eye, illuminating your psychic vision, begin!

৯৯৯

Bear in mind that spells may manifest literally or symbolically. For example, if you cast a spell asking for gold, you might receive a gold ring, a gold shirt, or even goldenseal! Also remember that you still have your part of the magick to do when the spell is complete, namely following up on mundane levels.

Last, but not least, when you see your spell manifest, remember to pat yourself on the back and be thankful for your blessings. A heart full of gratitude is always ready to give and receive magick.

Candle Charms, Amulets, Talismans, and Fetishes

We don't always think of candles as being used for these kinds of magick, but they certainly can be applied as such with a little creativity. To make candle charms and amulets, however, it helps to understand the subtle differences between these four methods.

Amulets are protective and have a preservative quality. The energy in the amulet remains neutral until called into play by circumstances or activated by the bearer. Thus, a house candle that you light when tensions or troubles arise is a good illustration of an amuletic candle.

Amuletic House Candle

If possible, have everyone in your household participate in the creation and blessing of a house candle. I strongly suggest making the candle square or house-shaped. The square symbolizes foundations, and the house shape represents the home in literal and figurative terms. Pick out a protective aromatics to add to the wax, such as cedar or bay, and other scents to stress love and harmony like rose or lavender, respectively. Create your house candle on a Thursday to inspire devotion or a Friday to stress overall positive relationships.

Once the candle is cooled completely, put it in a special place of honor in your home. Afterward, everyone involved in making the candle should stand in front of it holding hands and saying, "Protect and bring peace, let our spell ne'r cease. When the candle ignites our magick takes flight!" Keep repeating this incantation until the energy in the room hums with positive power. Light the candle and let it burn for a short time, then blow it out. Light it again any time there seems to be the need for protection or decreased stress in the home.

Charms

Charms are an active form of magick in that their energy is always "on" (most of us don't want to deter good things!), and they can have three distinct roles in candle spells:

1. As verbal commands akin to an incantation,
2. As the physical outcome of a magickal method aimed at attracting good energy and keeping evil at bay (similar to the amuletic candle, only with a different focus),
3. As a word or phrase carved into the candle itself.

Because many people want to carry charms to receive the most benefit from them, it might be wise to design your candle charms out of birthday candles, floating candles, or other smaller tapers.

Candle Charm for Luck

For this charm I suggest you save a candle from your birthday cake or some other special occasion that has a positive association for you. The birthday candle in particular houses all the good feelings and wishes of friends and family, so it has all the right energy to help inspire luck.

Next, take a toothpick and carve a lucky emblem into the candle carefully so as not to break it. One good choice is the rune Sowelu, which looks like a lightening bolt and represents the blessings and fortune of the sun. Dab this image with a bit of personal cologne or perfume as you focus on your goal of attracting luck. If you wish, add an incantation like, "Wherever I take this candle, luck will follow as well! When near me this candle shines, then good luck will surely be mine."

Wrap the candle in white cloth to protect it from breakage (this breaks the magick), and carry it with you regularly. Light it when you need luck to come quickly!

Fetishes

Fetishes represent some type of indwelling power, the energy of which is meant to be released at a specific time, or for specific purposes. Candles are excellent fetishes because they can be lit at a specific time, and can be used for just one working or several interconnected workings. To my thinking, however, in order for a candle to evoke a deep emotional reaction and really be energized, the fetish candle should be made by the practitioner. This will create sympathy and an intimate understanding of what that candle represents by the time the energy is required.

Talismans

Talismans are created during auspicious astrological times and energized with words of power. These words of power either saturate the talisman with ongoing energy, or act as a command phrase that will activate the talisman's power when most

Talisman of Banishing

Find a tiny black or dark blue candle. Wait until the moon is waning and nearly dark. Stand beneath the moon holding the candle skyward and say: "Evil away, only goodness may stay. By my will and my words, let my prayers be heard."

Put the candle in a fire-safe area and light it. Let it burn completely as you continue to repeat the incantation quietly. when the candle goes dark, turn and walk away. Do not look back as this symbolically accepts the negativity back.

needed. So you could create talismanic candles whose energy is ignited by the flame and a specific, pre-set "code" of words that also represents your need or goal.

༄·༄·༄

Even with all the options presented in this chapter, we have only scratched the surface of the multi-faceted art of candle magic in all its forms. For where there is spellcraft, there is often divination. Where there is divination, there is often a prayer. Where there is prayer, there is quiet introspection. All are somehow interconnected like the magick that powers them.

Prayers and 4 Meditations

The very act of lighting the candle is a prayer—my small
circle of light is a prayer.
—Brother David Steindl-Rast, *Gratefulness, the Heart of Prayer*

Buddhism provides a very good model for using candles as part of prayers or meditations. Here, the candle represents the light within each person, and the ability of the higher self to guide each soul from darkness to enlightenment. More than that, however, lighting the candle is a purposeful act. There is thought and will behind it. So as the candle flares, the focus is really on igniting our inner selves and motivating the special magick each one of us has at our disposal. In effect, it is not the action itself but the intention that really matters.

The lighting of a candle for meditation and prayer is really not so much for Spirit's sake as for ours. It signifies the desire to kindle something within, and to leave behind the mundane world, if only for a moment. And, when done repeatedly in either context, the candle lighting itself becomes a mini ritual that puts our mind and spirit into the right framework for what's ahead.

Candlelight Prayers

I think a lot of people are put off by the idea of praying. It reminds us of uncomfortable days in Sunday school or church, wiggling in our seats and reciting words that we didn't understand (and getting scolded if we didn't!). And even for those who have better memories of childhood prayers, there seems to be a part of the human creature that feels ill at ease in speaking to Spirit. This need not be so.

To pray is to open yourself to Spirit in truth and simplicity. It's a way to connect and stay connected with our spiritual nature. Prayer can also become a kind of attitude that doesn't have a specific time frame. A prayerful person is respectful and aware, and brings his or her soulful nature into everyday life. Better still, unlike some magical method, prayer is a technique you can use anywhere, anytime, without needing tools. All you need is you!

That said, candles do help us in prayer in many ways. For people who are having trouble turning their minds away from daily things, the candle is a good focus point. The softness of the light is a dramatic change from harsh florescent bulbs and other mundane things. By sitting in front of a candle in a dimly lit room, you will find that a lot of your tensions ease quite naturally and your attitude shifts. This, in turn, makes prayer easier.

Second, a prayer is (in some ways) a kind of incantation or invocation. So when a candle is lit during prayer, it represents a wish turned to the universe. It represents both your prayer and Spirit, to whom that prayer is directed.

Third, candles can have other symbolic value to prayers. For example, we light a candle to represent a person in need, or a spirit who has passed over, in the hopes of bringing that person aid or peace. This has been a custom in churches for hundreds of years and there's certainly no reason that it cannot translate into the church of our homes and hearts.

Effective Prayer

The next obvious question many people have is, "Okay, so how do I pray?" I'm going to outline a basic process here and provide some examples, but know that my approach to prayer and what works for you may be very different. Trust your instincts in this (and all spiritual matters) above what you read in any book.

1. Choose a candle. A plain white candle is traditional if you want it to symbolize Spirit. If praying for a person, you might want to have a second candle in his or her favorite color. If praying for something very personal, you might want to choose a second candle in a color that represents your goal.

2. Prepare the candle(s). If you want to carve it, dab it with oil, or simply bless it before you begin, do so. For example, many goddesses have the rose as a sacred flower. If the goddess you follow does, it might be nice to dab the white candle with rose oil to honor her. Note: just as with spellcraft, each of these steps defines your prayer in your own mind before you release it to Spirit.

3. Prepare yourself. Relax, go to someplace private, and still your mind. Remember: Spirit speaks in the still, silent moments of the soul.

4. Light the candle at the outset of the prayer, or at a point during the prayer that seems appropriate. Returning to our example of praying for someone else, it makes sense to light the individual's candle when you speak his or her name. This creates a stronger sympathetic connection between the individual and the candle.

5. Pray sincerely with words that are comfortable to you. This isn't the time to worry about the king's English! Trust me, Spirit will not correct your spelling or grammar. Just be yourself.

6. Be hopeful, trustful, humble, and reasonable. Socrates said that "God knows what's right for us," and sometimes that right thing isn't what we happen to think it should be.

7. Be thankful. This is among the most overlooked parts of nearly every spiritual process of which I know. People cast spells, say prayers, and then forget to be thankful when the energy finally manifests. Don't figuratively spit on the universe's gifts when they come—it's really bad karma and won't inspire quick manifestation with future requests.

You may be wondering what you should pray about. There are prayers of thanks, worshipful prayers, invoking prayers, and acknowledgment prayers. The thankful prayer is pretty forthright. It simply shows gratitude to the Powers for life, health, or the answer to a wish. Worshipful prayers honor the Sacred Parent and help us understand the importance of that Being in our lives. Invoking prayers act as an invitation for the Divine presence to share your sacred space, and acknowledgment prayers are simply those where we recognize and accept certain lessons, failings, and successes in our spiritual lives. What do you talk to good friends about, or wish you could? Spirit is a great listener, and prayer is just another way of communicating.

Creativity

In ancient Greek lore, the Muses were goddesses who presided over various areas of creativity. If you follow a Greek styled path, these would be ideal beings to whom to direct a prayer for creativity. As for color options, yellow is generally considered an inventive hue. Good dressings for the candle include wine, allspice oil, or lotus oil. (Note: You may want to bring your art with you to this prayer session, as people often find that ideas come quite rapidly afterward.)

Light the Spirit candle, saying:

> *Spirit of art and inspiration, I come to you.*
> *My vision seems short, and originality wanting.*
> *Release me from old, outmoded ways of thinking*
> *   and being.*
> *Refresh my spirit and soul.*
>
> *Even as I ignite this candle [light candle],*
> *Let inventiveness burn within me.*
> *Fill me with ideas, then let them pour out through*
> *   my [type of work or art].*
> *For the good of all, and it harm none, let it begin*
> *   today!*

After this prayer, it's a good idea to sit quietly in the light of the two candles and meditate. Clear your mind of anything other than you and Spirit, and let that connection and flow give you the kick-start you need.

Faith

Faith is an integral component to all religions and to our magick. If we don't trust in what we do, our actions become meaningless and powerless. Even so, there are many situations that stretch our faith to the limits, times when we find our trust waning. This is the perfect time to go to Spirit and pray for faith and hope.

The color of faith is silvery white (to me anyway), because it implies purity. Alternative colors used for matters of devotion include pale yellow and harvest orange. A good dressing for your candle is mint, lemon, or orange oil.

Light a large pillar or self-contained candle and settle your mind and heart. Open yourself to Spirit's flow, and recite the following prayer:

> *Great Spirit, I find myself feeling uncertain. My foundations are shaking; my path has grown rocky. I know there are times in every soul's life where tests come. If this is a test, help me accept it and give me the inner strength to endure. If it is not a test, turn the negative energies away that undermine my spirit. I have come to a crisis point, and I need to find that last ember of faith and trust on which to hold until things change. Shine a light on that ember; give it a greater glow so it lights a way during this dark time. Thank you.*

Let the candle burn unhindered, as it represents the flame of faith that burns within every soul, even when we have trouble seeing or sensing it.

Family Unity

Every family has its problems and pressures. These things can begin to wear away at the foundation of a family's harmony, however, if that base isn't constantly renewed and refreshed.

To my thinking the best time to pray for family unity is at the dinner table when everyone is gathered. This need not happen every day, but I do recommend it once a week. For a candle, you should have everyone help create a house candle. To do this, melt the wax and have each person add a significant ingredient that represents his or her wish for the family. In this manner, a properly made house candle represents each person (and pet) who lives under your roof and it also represents the spirit of the entire home.

Put this candle on the table at the center point (this provides balance). Light it and join hands, saying in unison:

> *Guide and protect us,*
> *Hold us and heal us,*
> *Strengthen and encourage us.*
> *Keep our family together*
>   *in the bond of love.*
> *So be it.*

Leave the candle burning throughout the meal, then put it away for another occasion.

Humor

Laughter is great medicine and an even better coping mechanism. Keeping one's funny bone in good working condition can make many difficult days seem a lot easier.

For this prayer I suggest picking out a candle that makes you laugh because of it's shape or color, or for whatever reason. Carve a big smile onto its surface using a feather, so you're symbolically tickling your fancy. Light it at the beginning of the prayer and say something like:

Spirit of the muse, of laughter and light, please bring on the giggles, the smiles, and fill me with joy until I overflow. Let me see the humor in even the most difficult of times, and let the strength of laughter walk with me on my path.

Take the candle into the living room and watch a good comedy flick!

Love

Humans are not solitary creatures. We do not survive healthily without positive emotional input. And of all the good emotions, love is the most powerful as a supportive, transforming tool. It is also one of the most important guiding forces for magick. A prayer for love is not selfish, it's necessary!

The colors of love vary. Pink is a gentle, friendly love, and red is a deeper, passionate love. Choose your hue accordingly. As for an aromatic, rose is the most predominant scent that's been associated with love in all its forms for ages. That strong association will give your prayer a positive boost of energy.

Take the chosen candle and carve a heart onto the surface around the mid-point. Set it into a holder, light it, and then say:

Gods and goddesses of love, pray hear my request. I have walked a solitary path for a very long time and am lonely. I need _____ (fill this in with a specific type of love like friendship, a lover, or whatever) *in my life. I need to be needed.*

My goal is not to manipulate another, nor to cling to another just because I've been alone. Instead, I want to build a partnership that's founded on trust, honesty, and spiritual understanding. Help bring the right person to me, be it the greatest good. So be it.

Let the candle continue to burn until it consumes the heart, then blow it out, letting the remaining smoke carry your wishes to the heavens.

Protection

By far one of the most common uses for candles throughout history was as symbols of safety because they gave light to the night. Therefore, using a candle during a prayer for protection is very apt. The traditional color for protection is white, and the aromatics for protection are abundant. The choices include cedar, clove, frankincense, lilac, lotus, raspberry, and violet.

You may want to check to see if any of these (or other) protective scents have a specific function. For example, cedar is often used to safeguard health. And although health can be literal (physical), the concept could also be extended to safeguard the health of a relationship.

I also suggest bringing a representation of the person, situation, pet, or thing that you're trying to protect. This gives you a focal point. Put that item under or near the candle so it benefits the most from the resulting energy. Leave the candle unlit until you name the person or situation in your prayer, which might go like this:

[Name of your personal god or goddess] watch over _____. [Light the candle]. Let the light of Spirit surround and protect him/her wherever he/she goes. Guide his/her footsteps; lead him/her away from danger; let him/her never want. Grant peace and harmony to ____'s spirit, let understanding fill his/her mind, and bring healing to his/her body. While we are apart, let your safety and my love hold him/her close and keep him/her well. So be it.

Spirits of the Dead

It is quite common for people to light candles on behalf of someone who has passed over. The reasons for this vary. In some instances it's a prayer to bring that spirit rest. In other cases it acts as a kind of memorial to the deceased, specifically on the day of his birth or death. In other scenarios still, the candle is like an invocation to that spirit to come and commune with the living. Whatever the case is for you, the prayer should be reflective of the purpose.

White candles or red candles are often used for all of these tasks, white representing the spirit and red representing the eternal living nature of the soul. Alternatively, a color might be chosen that was the person's favorite in life. Similarly, the aromatic chosen is often that of a perfume or cologne that the deceased often wore.

Interesting Fact

Many individuals who feel they've experienced the presence of a ghost say that the first sign was an aroma wafting through the room. Sometimes the aroma was that of flowers, but frequently it was the scent of the person's perfume or cologne!

This prayer is suited to the task of invocation:

Great Spirit, who past and present sees, Master of the veil between the worlds, I implore you. Bring the spirit of _____ *to the edge of our human realm this day. Let him/her share in this sacred space, in order that* _____ [Specify your purpose here. For people who had unfinished business, this is a good chance to heal some unresolved wounds or say farewell properly. On other occasions, like a wedding, it's a chance for the ancestors to rejoice in our happiness]. *If the spirit has moved on to a new life, however, send them my love and good wishes, with my thanks and desire to do no harm. So be it.*

Sit in the light of the candle for some time in a meditative frame of mind. If a spirit is going to come to you, it may do so now in the safety of a sacred space, or possibly later in a dream.

Work

Employment is very important to our overall well-being. It provides financial security and a sense of accomplishment. When there are problems with an employment situation, or one cannot find work, the ensuing stress creates all kinds of trouble, for which a little divine intervention wouldn't hurt.

The color for work-oriented candles can be green or gold (for money) or perhaps brown (to represent strong foundations). This candle might be carved with an emblem that represents your career—for me it would be a pen, for a carpenter it might be a hammer or nail, and so forth.

Light the candle at the opening of the prayer, saying:

This light is my hope for better days. Let the stress associated with _____ [describe your situation in detail] *wane. Let the negativity associated with this situation stay buried in the past. Help me regain my professional confidence so I can apply myself more effectively in my work.*

Also help me grow in my career so I don't stagnate mentally or physically. I thank you for the providence this job has given me and my family so far, and ask that it, or something similarly suited to my skills, continue to care for us. Let prosperity and peace reign at work and at home. So be it.

Let this candle burn down to the carved image, then save the rest for another work-related prayer, ritual, or spell.

Candle Meditations

I've spoken in some detail about the way candlelight seems to change the way we feel and react. And even though most people meditate with their eyes closed, beginning a meditation by focusing on a candle can really help set the tone for everything that's to come. When we light a candle before meditation, we designate the space as something special, something sacred. Within the sphere of the candle's beams we create a reality in our mind's eye that can have truly amazing transforming powers.

Effective Meditation

St. Ambrose, who lived in 340 A.D., said quite wisely that "Meditation is the eye wherewith we see God." More than that, however, meditation is an important time of introspection and integration. It is a time when we stop for a moment and really think about what is, was, and will be. Better still, meditation is relaxing, focusing, and clarifying. But not everyone finds it easy to meditate. Why?

Well, honestly, humans tend to think of dozens of things all at the same time. While we're writing a grocery list, we might also be thinking about laundry, the budget, the kids, or whatever. Meditation requires that we stop our rushing for a moment, and still all other thoughts save for the matter at hand. In fact, some meditative practices strive to empty the mind of thought all together to allow the individual to simply be. So, if you find yourself feeling a little antsy about meditating, don't worry—you're not alone!

This guideline, however, should help:

10 Steps to Effective Candlelight Meditations

1. Find a private place where you won't be bothered by people, pets, or other interruptions.

2. Make sure this place has a comfortable sitting or lying area (I suggest sitting so you don't fall asleep).

3. Get comfortable. You don't have to look like a pretzel for meditation to work. In fact, it probably won't work if you feel completely awkward.

4. Light whatever candle you've chosen to represent the theme of your meditation. (Just as with prayers, the color, aroma, and carvings on the candle can symbolize your goals.)

5. Look at the candle and just enjoy watching it for a few minutes. Stretch out your neck. Wiggle. Readjust your positioning until you feel wholly at ease.

6. Begin breathing at a slow, even pace. This helps relieve tension so you can focus your mind more readily.

7. Continue looking toward the candle, but not directly at it. Let everything around you become fuzzy. At some point, your eyes will quite naturally close.

8. See the candle still burning in your mind's eye. The glow surrounds and protects you in this quiet time. Know that it will be there even when your visualization/meditation takes you elsewhere.

9. Begin the actual visualization/meditation (examples of which follow).

10. Make notes of your feelings, any images that come to you, and other parts of your experience. These will prove useful later when you're putting together other meditations for yourself.

Expectations vs. Reality

No one becomes an expert at meditation over night. It takes time and practice. It's best to start out slowly. Try to simply sit quietly for five minutes. Believe me, for most people this will prove quite difficult enough! As you get better at it, begin increasing the time you meditate to about a total of 20 or 30 minutes, for the greatest benefit.

Additionally, try not to go into any meditation with preset expectations. For example, people who use meditation as a way of finding an animal totem or guide (discussed later this chapter) should not anticipate a particular animal showing up. This can skew the experience and may even deter the "right" creature because it feels unwelcome. Likewise, someone who uses a meditation to contact a ghost or spirit and expects a particular response might actually mentally *create* that response. Releasing our expectations, therefore, improves the reliability of our experiences.

You will notice that these meditations don't simply instruct a person to sit and think. I've added imagery (visualization) and sometimes a chant to increase the sensual cues you receive. Beyond this, you can certainly play soft music and burn incense if you find the sounds or aromas help to further focus your spirit toward the task at hand.

Animal Totems and Guides

Meditating to find an animal totem or spirit guide is something found in shamanic traditions. Magickal practitioners have adopted this idea because most of us have a strong affinity with the natural world and recognize the benefits of connecting with animal guides. You see, the spiritual essence of various creatures usually come to a person when that creature's attributes are most needed. Alternatively, the animal may represent an important part of an individual's personality. In both cases, this being can become a great magickal helpmate, from whom good insights and lessons come.

This candle meditation is designed to help you discover an animal guide of which you may be unaware, or to better connect with one that's already appeared to you. I suggest using colors from nature—dark green or brown—for the candle, and aromatics that also make you feel like you're in a natural setting (pine, clover, and so on). Better still, if you can perform this meditation in a remote location, the results often improve.

Light the candle and get comfortable. Breathe deeply and evenly and look at the candle's flame. Let the light from the candle reach out and hold you. Let it become part of your aura and surroundings. You'll know you've done this right if you start feeling a little warmer. This light acts as a protective sphere for the meditation.

After you feel centered and relaxed, close your eyes. In your imagination, see the light of the candle still glowing. Whisper to the energy of this light, telling it your desire to meet one of your animal guides. Use words with which you're comfortable—this is akin to an invocation or prayer.

Let the vision of the light begin to swirl and twist until images start to appear. The image will be of some natural location (this might be the sea, a forest, the desert, or whatever area the animal spirit feels most comfortable in). Repeat your request again. You do not need to speak out loud. Most animal spirits communicate empathically or telepathically anyway.

Stay in this meditative state for a while, and wait patiently. If an animal does not appear, it might come to you later in a dream (which for most people is when we're most receptive to spiritual input). If one does appear, pay particular attention to (a) what it is, and (b) what it does, and write that down somewhere. You'll want to remember it and study it for insights afterward.

Sometimes the creature will communicate a message, and it might even tell you its name. Again, remember these things. Even if they don't make sense right now, they may later on (even months and years from now).

At some point, the animal will simply depart. This signals the end of your time together, but you can always return. The animal may or may not come every time you enact this meditation, but you've established a meeting spot and rapport that won't be easily broken.

Cleansing and Purification

For those moments when you have no sage or cedar to move through your aura, when you can't take a relaxing bath in cleansing herbs, and the only tool you have is a candle—have no fear! This is still a perfectly good implement to use in a purification meditation. In fact, the element of fire is associated with cleansing anyway. All you'll be doing is applying that association a little more personally.

The color of purity is white. The aromatics connected to cleansing and purification include frankincense, myrrh, bay, lemon, and mint. If you'd like to consider special timing for this meditation, work during the dark moon—the traditional time to weed things out of our lives (in this case unwanted energies).

Begin as before by lighting the candle and getting comfortable. Welcome the warm light of the candle into your aura. See it slowly expand from the small flame in front of you to a glow that reaches out and saturates the entire room. When you have this image firmly in mind, close your eyes.

Continue the imagery but now add an extra dimension. See the candlelight sparkling all around you, as if there were tiny fireflies everywhere. These small particles of light move in to ward your being as you inhale. From the air in your lungs, they travel through the blood to every cell in your body, collecting negativity and cleansing as they go. After a moment, when you exhale, they return out, no longer bright and shiny but brown. Let these drop to the earth to be absorbed.

Repeat this process of inhaling cleansing fire and exhaling dirt until the light that goes in is just as bright as the light that comes out. This means you've accomplished as much as you can in one sitting. Let your breathing return to normal. Open your eyes, make notes of your experience, and blow out the candle. Keep it handy for another cleansing meditation or a purifying/banishing spell.

Dream work

Dreams are very important to the human psychological makeup. They can also be a vehicle through which ghosts, our higher self, and Spirit can speak to us. Why dreams? Because when we sleep, our minds aren't busy doing quite so much. We slow down, it's quiet, and therefore we are more open to subtle input.

What color you associate with dreams might be rather personal (dream work is, by it's nature, subjective). I always think of them as pale blue for some reason. Aromatics associated with inspiring dreams include jasmine, rose, and marigold. Other things sensual cues that you might find helpful include playing soft music (with bells or another sound that you find centering), and lying on a soft, comfortable surface. This is one meditation where it's okay to fall asleep, so long as you have a fire-safe location for your candle.

Bring a notebook and pen to the area where you plan to try this meditation, or perhaps a tape recorder so you can mark down the results immediately upon waking. Light the candle and lie down. Make sure you can see the candlelight easily from where you are. Dimming the lights in the room helps, as does working at night and/or during the full moon, which represents inspiration.

As you look toward the candle, quietly repeat this chant:

> *I am the light,*
> *The light is within,*
> *The light awakens my dreams,*
> *Let the magick begin.*

You may notice that the chant has a tendency to start out quiet, get louder, then settle back down again. This is normal. It's a way of raising energy, so if it happens, don't stifle that instinct.

Continue watching the candle, breathing evenly, and repeating the chant until you feel yourself drifting off. Don't fight sleep. Let yourself relax wholly. Give yourself over to the sacred sleep time. When you awaken, immediately write down anything that you can recall. Dreams can disappear very quickly in waking hours, so don't wait! You can worry about the meaning later. Think about as many details as possible: colors, smells, people, repeated imagery, and so forth. Then, when time allows, look up the information in a good dream interpretation guide.

Energy Increase

I don't know about you, but there are days when I feel totally "unplugged"— as if my battery were dead. Meditation can help relieve this drained sensation and also help reconnect you to the life energy that's all around you everyday.

For this meditation I recommend surrounding yourself with candles. Either put one at each of the points of the compass (North, South, East, and West), or in a circle around you. The color for energy is usually red, but if you choose a compass configuration, you may want to use elementally colored candles. These are blue for West/Water, green or brown for North/Earth, yellow for East/Air, and red or orange for South/Fire. Both options create a semi-formal sacred space for your meditation, especially when accompanied by verbalization of intent. Here are sample invocations for both choices of candle configurations:

Elemental: Light the candle associated with each element as you come to the verse that honors it.

> *I welcome the Air and its creative energy.*
> *I welcome the Fire and its passionate energy.*
> *I welcome the Water and its healing energy.*
> *I welcome the Earth and its motivational energy.*
> *I with them; they in me,*
> *So mote it be.*

Circle: Light the candles moving clockwise, repeating this invocation as often as necessary to go around the entire circuit once.

> *The circle is around, above, and below,*
> *And where it abides, magick and power grow.*
> *Banish fatigue and apathy,*
> *Replace them with abundant energy!*

At the end of either of these invocations, sit in the middle of the candles and relax. Extend your senses so you can feel the warmth and power of the candles on the edge of your awareness. You will know you're doing this meditation correctly when you begin feeling somewhat hot (heat comes from energy!). Let this energy fill your aura until you feel as if you will burst, then return to your normal level of awareness.

Leave the candles burning so they support the meditation for a while longer, or blow them out in reverse order from when you lit them to release the sacred space.

Protection

The light in the darkness; the light that banishes shadows; the light that we associate with the safety of the Sacred— the candle embodies this symbolism. Think of the pumpkin at Halloween. The light shining from within is a candle, and it's meant to protect against malicious or mischievous spirits. Well, what about the light that shines within each one of us? Couldn't a candle meditation activate the same kind of protective power? Sure it can!

Traditionally the color of protection is white. The aromatics may depend on the specific area of trouble. Some general protective scents include violet and myrrh. Use a large, enclosed pillar candle for this meditation, and light it at the outset.

Sit in front of the candle and let yourself absorb its warmth. Look toward the candle until you know you can see the light that extends from the candle in your mind's eye (not the flame, but the glow). At this point, close your eyes and continue breathing deeply. See that glow beginning to form a shell all around you. Make sure the light extends below your feet and above your head in a three-dimensional globe. When the globe is fully formed, you will likely feel a little different (set apart), and the room may even seem quieter.

You can take this globe with you anywhere (it rolls!). You need not dispel it at the end of the meditation. And, you can also create it in your mind's eye at any time, with or without candles to help the process along.

જાજાજી

As you can see, the potential for using candles in prayer and meditation is pretty open-ended. Candles are wonderful, inexpensive helpmates that don't require an invitation to come and help you in magick!

5
Rituals

The Cardinal rose with a dignified look he call'd for his candle,
his bell, and his book.
—Richard Harris Barham, *The Jackdaw of Rheims*

Anyone who has ever been to church is familiar with the custom of lighting candles for various reasons. And although the symbolic value of candle lighting is a little different in Christian tradition than it is in Wicca, there are commonalities worth exploring. Why? Because these commonalities speak to us of the underlying truths that can bring more power and symbolic value to our rituals.

A 15th-century writer by the name of Simeon of Thessalonica said that pure wax represented a pure heart when it was lit. To him, offering a candle symbolized a person's desire to reconnect with the Divine. Similarly, in Wicca, white candles are often used to represent pure Spirit or pure intentions (as in a wedding ritual), and the candle flame is often used for meditative purposes to reconnect ourselves with the Divine. In Catholicism candles are lit as a prayer for the dead, or when the health of a loved one is wavering. In Wicca, we often include a candle to honor our ancestors, and we burn specifically colored or scented candles in spells and rituals for health. I could go on, but I think you get the idea. Simply put, candles were, and are, an important part of religious rituals.

The Colors of Magick

Focusing more specifically on Neo-Pagan and magickal traditions, the color of a candle has often been nearly as important as the candle itself in a ritual construct. We have already discussed the applications for color in spells, prayers, and meditations, but because I've noticed some minor shifts in color symbolism for ritual, I wanted to include a list here. Please note, however, that the associations sometimes change depending on one's cultural path. I've listed here the most common meanings as a starting point:

Candle Colors for Ritual Purposes

Blue: The Western quarter of a circle, representing Water, peacefulness, joy, and intuition.

Brown: Grounding, good foundations, Earth magick (an alternative color for the Northern quarter). Winter rituals.

Gold: The sun, the masculine aspect, power, leadership (alternative colors are yellow or red).

Green: The Northern quarter of a circle, representing Earth, growth, foundations, and cycles. Spring rituals.

Orange: Victory, hospitality, emotional warmth. Fall rituals.

Pink: Well-being, devotion, friendship.

Purple: Spirituality, leadership, psychism.

Red: The Southern quarter of a circle, representing Fire, energy, love, passion, and dramatic transformation. Summer rituals.

White: Spirit, purity, the moon, sincerity, the Goddess. Considered an all-purpose color when other candles aren't available. An alternative color is silver.

Yellow: The Eastern quarter of a circle, representing Air, communication, divination, the mind, and movement.

To further improve the symbolic value, combine the candle's color with an aroma by either burning incense or anointing the candle. Some good combinations include:

The Scent of Colors

Black: Clove, juniper, frankincense.

Blue: Lavender, violet, lilac.

Brown: Honeysuckle, patchouli, vervain.

Green: Pine, vetivert, primrose.

Orange: Peach, pineapple.

Pink: Rose, amber, lemon.

Purple: Jasmine, thyme, myrrh, sandalwood.

Red: Vanilla, rose, patchouli.

White: Sandalwood, sage, frankincense and myrrh (combined).

Yellow: Rosemary, anise, orange.

Note that these combinations are geared only to the general vibrations of a candle's colors. You should always fine-tune and mix and match your aromatics to match specific goals whenever possible. To this end, I recommend getting a good book on herbalism. In particular my *Herbal Arts* and Paul Beyerl's *Herbal Magick* should be of help.

Elements of Effective Ritual

Rituals are a formal way of honoring the sacred, commemorating a special moment, and creating a sacred space within which we can work our magick. Yet many people feel awkward about ritual and really don't know where to begin. The first step is simply accepting the fact that many parts of your life are already mini-rituals. If you follow the same routine every day, if you drive the same route to work, if you use a specific cup for tea, these are all rituals. The repetition of an action provides comfort and familiarity—the same kind of comfort and familiarity that we would like to achieve with our magick some day.

The next step is to think about what ritual, in general terms, achieves. Ritual is ultimately a way to connect the physical to the metaphysical and fulfill our connection to the Sacred. But for a ritual to create that kind of fulfillment, it has to have a construct that builds energy, that builds on the pattern of life itself.

So what exactly is an effective ritual construct? It is one that gently and sensitively creates from nothing the right magick for the task at hand. To achieve this goal, most rituals follow this kind of pattern:

1. The gathering of materials (words, props, incense, clothing, etc.) that accent the ritual's theme.

2. Consecrating these materials for the task at hand.

3. Self-preparation (mental, physical, and spiritual).

4. Going to the space in which the ritual will take place and setting it up to reflect that ritual.

5. Creating sacred space by calling the Quarters and inviting the Sacred into attendance (there will be many examples of this in this chapter).
6. Bringing as many senses as possible into the ritual process through the use of props and techniques.
7. Creating a rhythm of movement, word, and energy that pulses and vibrates in the spirits of all gathered.
8. Releasing that energy toward its goal after it has reached its pinnacle.
9. Grounding the residual energy and dismissing the sacred space (this provides closure).
10. Integrating the experience. For future reference, it helps to make notes of what felt right.

Let's look at each of these points briefly. Point 1 is necessary because otherwise the ritual might be disrupted by the need to go get a component. As you're choosing these things, try to have something that stimulates each sense (point 6), as each piece of sensory input greatly improves the results achieved. More importantly, the process of thinking about and gathering special items for the ritual focuses your mind and charges those components with good energy. This energy, in turn, eases the consecration process (point 2), so that each item participating in the ritual is vibrating at the best possible level to support the working.

Perhaps the most important step is self-preparation. Ritual is a sacred act, and it should be approached with proper groundwork in place. This doesn't mean making the entire process into something drab and depressing, but it does mean thinking a bit about what we're doing and why we're doing it.

At this juncture some kind of purification is appropriate. Some people abstain from sex or specific foods before a ritual, for example. Others take a ritual bath or smudge their aura with sage smoke. Beyond spiritual purification, it's also a good idea to try to eat natural foods, get plenty of rest, and drink plenty of water the day before a ritual. This cleanses the body, clears the mind, and allows magick to flow through an unhindered channel.

Now it's time to go to wherever the ritual will be held, taking everything you need with you. When you arrive, don't just go bounding into the area, but walk into it gently with a prayerful attitude. Set everything up thoughtfully so that each item is safe, easy to reach, and in an appropriate location for its function. Also put the items in a location that accents their sensual application (for example, if you have something that's meant to stimulate touch, have it close enough to touch).

For point 7, the creating of a sacred space usually includes an invocation of some kind to the four elemental powers (Earth, Air, Fire, and Water). This proceeds around the circle clockwise for most rituals, and counterclockwise for banishing or lessening magicks. A prayer to Spirit or a statement of purpose is also common. As with all parts of the ritual, the invocation and prayer reflect the theme of the rite. Take your time with this, as it is perhaps the most important part of a ritual in that it sets apart the mundane from the metaphysical for us, and in spiritual space.

By the way, for those of you who may not be familiar with some of the common associations for the four directions and elements, it helps to have this information handy. You can begin or end invocations or spells in a specific quarter of the sacred space to accent a specific type of energy (the focus of the ritual). You can also enact other special activities at that quarter point to support your efforts. Here's a brief correspondence list to which to refer:

Direction/Element	Correspondences
North/Earth	Financial matters, security, grounding, foundations, steady growth/change, Earth magick.
East/Air	Communication, transformation, movement, humor, inventiveness, wind magick.
South/Fire	Purification, illumination, the God aspect, energy, passion, consciousness, sun and Fire magick.
West/Water	Intuition, healing, cleansing, peace, nurturing, unconscious, the Goddess aspect, moon and Water magick.

After creating sacred space, the exact body of the ritual also varies, but the keynote is building power for your specific theme/purpose. This brings us to releasing the energy. Magick will do little good if you don't send it on its way. Like an arrow in a bow, it needs to fly! Many people in Wicca accomplish this by a loud clap or a physical movement that cuts the energy free.

At the close of everything, it's important to take time for grounding and releasing the sacred space. Magick can leave you feeling light-headed or fuzzy, especially after a long ritual. And just as you wouldn't expect a guest in your home to tarry forever, releasing the sacred space provides closure for both you and the Powers.

Last, but certainly not least, write down what you most like and dislike about a ritual. What really felt right? What do you want to use again? What fell flat? Having these kinds of notes will produce much more effective rituals in the future.

Binding Ritual

What you'll need: a homemade candle with a knotted wick. To make the knotted wick, simply tie equally spaced knots in a wick prior to dipping or molding. Make sure you keep a strong image in your mind of which energies, person, or situation you intend to bind in the ritual. Adding a specific incantation can help too. For example, if you're going to bind negative energy during the ritual, you might say, *"Negativity away, only good energy stay,"* or perhaps, *"it is not this wick I bind, but* _____ (fill in appropriate word or phrase)." Repeat this as you tie each knot.

As for colors and aromatics, black wax is the traditional color of banishing and it is often used for binding (grounding) too. Any cleansing scents, like clove or lemon, are appropriate. Additionally it's nice to have incense, your magickal tools (like an athame, chalice, or whatever else you work with), and some soothing music for ritual to set the tone. Remember that no matter the setting, words, or actions of a ritual, it's really your outlook toward the moment that changes everything and makes the magick happen. Everything else is icing in the proverbial cake!

Setting up the space: At the outset of the ritual you will want the binding/banishing candle lit and placed in a central location, such as the top of an altar or a table, along with any other tools and adornments you've chosen. There will be no quarter candles in this ritual (those placed at North, South, East, and West), as the idea is to turn away energy rather than attract it.

The Invocation: Because this is a banishing ritual, we begin in the North and move to the East counterclockwise. Stand at the northern region of your sacred space and say:

> *Powers of the North, I call and charge you.*
> *Protect this sacred space and my magick.*
> *Take the negativity that has haunted me*
> *And bury it in your rich soils so something*
> *Good may grow in its place.*

Move to the western part of the circle, visualizing a bright white line of light connecting the two points, and say:

> *Powers of the West, I call and charge you.*
> *Protect this sacred space and my magick.*
> *Take the negativity that has washed upon my*
>   *shores*
> *And cleanse it away with your healing waves.*

Move to the southern part of the circle, continuing your visualization, and say:

> *Powers of the South, I call and charge you.*
> *Protect this sacred space and my magick.*
> *Take the negativity that has darkened my doorstep*
> *And banish it with your light.*

Move to the eastern part of the circle, now seeing the entirety of the space surrounded by white light in your mind's eye, and say:

> *Powers of the East, I call and charge you.*
> *Protect this sacred space and my magick.*
> *Take the negativity that storms through my life*
> *And move it away on the winds of change.*

Approach the center point of your circle, where the candle remains lit, and say:

Spirit, you are the light of the world.
When you are present, no darkness can abide.
My life has been troubled lately, and filled with
Energies that bind my joy and growth.
I come to you today and ask for positive change.
Bless the work of my hands this day,
And help me create a better tomorrow.
So be it.

As you stand before the candle, again think back to the situation that you wish to bind. Think back to making the knotted candle and tying your magick into those knots. Focus on this wholly until the flame burns one of the knots completely as you watch. As the knot first begins to flame, start chanting:

Burn away, burn away,
Only goodness may stay!

When the knot is completely consumed, blow out the candle. You can keep it for other similar rituals and spells.

Other Activities: At this juncture you can spend some time in the sacred space if you wish, reading or maybe using your incense to cleanse your aura. To accomplish this, take a feather or hand-held fan and move the smoke so it goes around you (counterclockwise), collecting any residual unwanted energy and taking it on the winds.

Another possible activity is a self blessing. Very often when there's been a lot of stress in someone's life, a blessing goes a long way to easing some of the agitation. Self blessings take many forms. One is that of dabbing a little favorite oil on various energy centers (chakras) while incanting. An example for the heart center might be, *"Bless my heart that it might heal, and be ready to give and receive love again."*

Closing: To close, you will be reversing the order of the invocation with these variations (beginning in the East):

Guardians of the East, I thank you.
Your winds have come and change has begun.
Hail and farewell.

Move to the South, visualizing the lines of energy from the opening of the ritual slowly coming apart and disappearing as you move.

Guardians of the South, I thank you.
Your fires have burned away the darkness, and
    gifted me with hope.
Hail and farewell.

Move to the West, continuing the visualization:

Guardians of the West, I thank you.
Your waters flow to my soul and make me whole.
Hail and farewell.

Move to the North, now seeing the final lines of energy disappear in your mind's eye, and say:

Guardians of the North, I thank you.
Your soil gives me foundations in which to build
    anew.
Hail and farewell.

Move to the center and thank Spirit in any way you feel appropriate, then make notes of your experience in a magickal journal for future reference. Take hope from this place with you in your heart to greet the new day!

Luck-Changing Ritual

When things seem to be going badly and ill fortune finds you everywhere, this ritual is designed to help.

What you'll need: Pick out one or several candles in a color that you consider to represent luck. If you decide to use more than one candle, the number should be your lucky number. Aromatics suited to good fortune include allspice, heather, orange, pineapple, and violet. Alternatively, because this is a personal spell, you could dab some favorite perfume or cologne on the candle(s).

Additionally, it helps to carve the image of a four-leaf clover or other emblem that represents luck to you in one of the candles. Turn the candle upside down and carve the image into it while focusing on your goal (the reason for this will become apparent in the ritual). I find using a toothpick works nicely and avoids breaking thinner candles.

Setting up the space: Place the carved candle in the center of the circle with your tools. Any other candles can go at the four quarters or any other spot that is personally pleasing. You might also want to consider bringing any personal good luck charms into the space so they absorb the energy.

Invocation: This invocation moves clockwise (to attract positive energy). It begins in the East, which is the direction of movement and change (the Air element). Air is also something invigorating. It can inspire new thoughts and positive action that can bring about the serendipity that we so desperately need sometimes. If you've placed a candle in the East, you should light it as you say:

> *Master of the winds, let the magick begin.*
> *As I stand at the gate, let all bad luck abate!*

Move to the southern part of the sacred space, and light any candle you may have positioned there, saying:

> *Father Fire, let the energy raise higher.*
> *Let my spirit burn free, lit with serendipity!*

Move to the western part of the sacred space, lighting any candles you may have placed there, saying:

Sister rain, fill me again.
Born by the seas, bring good fortune to me!

Move to the northern part of the sacred space, lighting any candles you may have positioned there, saying:

Mother Earth, give the magick to birth.
Rooted in your rich ground, let luck in my spirit
abound!

Move to the center of the circle, where the carved candle is already burning. Take a deep breath and focus your will on turning away the negative tide. Reach out to grasp the candle near where the carving is, saying:

Bad luck turn, the candle no longer burns.

Turn the candle upside down (now the image of luck that you carved earlier is right side up!). Say:

When this new light shines, good luck will be mine.

Light the other end of the candle (note that you may need to carve this end back a little bit prior to the ritual so it's easy to light).

This entire process is akin to turning over an hourglass—the idea is to turn energy from what has been to what you need, making a negative into a positive. The ritual comes from an old gypsy trick used to turn attention elsewhere, but can easily be used for this purpose.

Other Activities: Since the entire ritual is designed to attract good fortune, this is an ideal time to make a lucky candle charm that you can take with you anywhere. Go back to Chapter 2 and read over the candle charm provided. Make personally pleasing changes and remember to bring what you need to the sacred space so you can create the charm while the magickal energy is at its peak.

You might also try other "turning" tricks. For example, some gamblers have been known to turn their socks inside out or sit backward on a chair to change luck. Each of these actions is a kind of sympathetic magick that supports your goal.

Closing: You will be releasing the energy of the sacred space in opposite order to where you began, starting in the North:

> *The seed has been planted; the work is begun,*
> *I thank you and bid you farewell.*

Blow out any candles in the North, then move to the West:

> *The water's flow is never ending; a new cycle is*
> *   begun.*
> *I thank you and bid you farewell.*

Blow out any candles here, then move to the South:

> *The fires of spirit burn; a new hearth is ignited.*
> *I thank you and bid you farewell.*

Again, blow out the candles here, and finish in the East, saying:

> *The winds grow still, but the magick continues,*
> *I thank you and bid you farewell.*

If you wish you can add a personal note of thanks to Spirit at this point.

Money-Drawing Ritual

Although we might often wish it were not so, the dollar has a lot of power in and around our lives. When we don't have enough money to pay our bills and maintain our lives adequately, it's very hard to focus on matters of spirit. That's where this ritual can help.

Note, however, that I caution against doing money-drawing rituals without forethought, as they can have interesting results. For example, many people report that they often get called on to work a lot of overtime or receive extra assignments shortly after working this ritual. Why? Because the universe expects us to maintain our role as co-creators and be willing to do some of the work necessary to meet our needs. Better still, we feel better about the results because we can see what comes from working with a joyful heart.

What you'll need: First, if possible wait until the three days of a full moon and repeat this ritual on each of the three days (any time is fine). The full moon represents abundance. Alternatively, work during the noon hour, when the sun shines brightly. The color of the sun accents prosperity (gold) and the light represents blessing.

Next, get three small green candles (one for each day) and carve several dollar signs into each on all sides. Rub a little mint, pine, or cinnamon oil into the images. Find gold, silver, or green candle holders to accent your goal or perhaps place the candle holders on top of a large bill ($50 or $100). Get an expensive bottle of wine or another beverage that you wouldn't normally buy for yourself and have it ready, along with a cup.

Setting up the space: Put one green candle at the center of the sacred space each day, along with the cup and one third of the beverage. Any other embellishments are purely personal, but I like to put a silver- or gold-toned coin at each of the quarters as I invoke them to surround myself with money.

Invocation: Money is associated with the Earth element, or northern quarter of the circle, so we will begin the invocation there, moving clockwise:

> *Mother of all abundance, I welcome you and ask
> for your aid.*

Lay down the coin then move to the East:

> *Winds of luck, I welcome you and ask for your aid.*

Lay down the coin and move to the South:

> *Fires of motivation, I welcome you and ask for your aid.*

Lay down the coin and move to the West:

> *Waters of plenty, I welcome you and ask for your aid.*

Move to the center, where you've placed the green candle. Light the candle, saying:

> *See my need; see my burden.*
> *By my will and my magick,*
> *Bring money by the next full moon.*

Wave the lit candle over the cup, saying:

> *I accept the fullness of blessing that is coming to me,*
> *And give thanks for what I have.*

Drink all the beverage except for a few drops, which should be poured to the Earth as a libation as you say:

> *Receive to give; give to receive.*

Repeat this activity each of the three days. Give the coins used in this ritual away to a worthy cause (do *not* keep them, as that will delay the magick's manifestation). By the next full moon, circumstances should be improving.

Other activities: There are two ways of attracting and drawing things to yourself that are quite common in Wicca. The first is to write the name of what you need on a piece of paper. This paper gets folded inward thrice, then bound by a long string. Place the paper across the table from you (beyond the green candle) and focus on your need. Slowly draw the paper into your hands using the excess string. When it arrives, tie it with the remaining thread and carry it as a prosperity charm until the money manifests. At this time the charm should be burned with a thankful heart.

A second method frequently used is to bind a magnet to a silver coin or a dollar bill so that the magnet attracts more of the same. This charm should be made in the sacred space and carried in or near a wallet.

Closing: This is a nice brief closing that works (with minor variations) for nearly any ritual. Stand in the center of your space and say:

> *Earth and Air, Fire and Sea,*
> *Thank you for being here with me,*
> *For seeing and meeting the needs in my heart,*
> *Merry meet; merry part!*

Peace Ritual

There are few of us who can say we've never hurt someone else's feelings or lost our temper. The purpose of this ritual is to restore peace and harmony to a situation or relationship where animosity has begun to destroy things.

What you'll need: If you're performing this ritual to restore peace to a situation (like in the workplace), you'll need a small candle to represent that situation. If you're performing this ritual to restore harmony with a person or group, it's best to enact it *with* that person or group (each person needs a small candle).

If circumstances do not allow you to work with the person or group, then pick out a suitable candle to represent the person or group. Carve it with name(s) and dab it with aromatics that create a strong sympathy to that person or group. For example, if you have a friend with whom you've had a falling out, you might carve her name in the candle and dab it with a scent you know she likes.

The best generic color for peace is white (you can use a white cloth on the altar to accent this energy even more). Aromatics suited to this ritual include lavender, lilac, rose, and violet.

Setting up the space: Place the candles for this ritual in the northern part of the sacred space and light them. This is the region ruled by Earth, which can accept and ground out negativity. Have a small cup of water in the West, and a pale orange candle in the South (unlit). The rest of the sacred space can be set up in a personally pleasing manner.

Invocation: We're starting this invocation in the South and moving counterclockwise. South is the region of fire—the element that rules our anger. Moving counterclockwise symbolizes diminishing or banishing:

> *Fires of the South, burn gently this day* (light candle)
> *For it is my/our wish that anger give way.*

Move to the East and say:

> *I greet the powers and winds from the East*
> *To blow away negativity; anger cease!*

Move to the North and say:

> *Soils of Earth, hear my/our cry*
> *replace anger with understanding, by n' by!*

Move to the West and say:

> *Waters swell, waves to and fro*
> *where e'er you wash, let healing flow!*

Pick up the cup of water that you left at the West and take it to the center of the circle. Hold the bowl to the sky and bless it, saying:

Water nourishes
Water cleanses
Water inspires
Let it nourish my/our soul(s)
Cleanse away all negativity
And inspire peace.

Take this to the North, where the candle of your anger has burned, and pick up the candle, saying:

Cease now all anger, bitterness and blame,
My will and my word, I douse your flame!

Turn the candle flame down into the water and make sure it's completely out. After the ritual you should take this somewhere and bury it to likewise bury the anger.

Other activities: My favorite addition to this ritual begins with bringing a good sized plant pot into the sacred space filled with rich soil and a few flowering seeds. Rather than waiting till the end of the ritual to bury the candle, push it down into the bottom of the pot. As you do, push all your anger and bad feelings down to the candle. Above it, place the seed for a flowering plant, saying:

Mind well the law of three;
I freely release my negativity!
as above so below,
Where anger dwelled, now beauty grows!

By the time the plant sprouts you should notice several positive changes in the situation or relationship toward which this ritual was directed.

Closing: Begin in the West, moving clockwise, since now you're ready to accept blessings and positive energy:

Powers of the West—thank you for your cleansing
and healing.

Move to the North and say:

> *Powers of the North—thank you for grounding out my anger.*

Move to the East and say:

> *Powers of the East—thank you for motivating positive change.*

Move to the South and say:

> *Powers of the South—thank you for the spark of magick.*

Take hold of the orange candle and lift it skyward, saying:

> *Spirit—I am but a human with human faults.*
> *Today I have released the fire of my anger to the guardians*
> *And wish to leave it behind me.*
> *Help me to do so with a thankful heart.*
> *So be it.*

Blow out the candle. This can be kept as a Quarter candle.

Strength/Courage Ritual

The world is a complex place where we are often faced with difficult situations. Inner resolve is not always an easy commodity to come by! When you feel weak-kneed and lacking a backbone, this is a good ritual aimed at restoring courage and fortitude.

What you'll need: A candle whose color represents courage to you (red is common), dabbed with cedar or musk oil to augment the energy. Also a piece of paper with the words "strength" and "courage" written upon it.

Setting up the space: Light the candle and put it in the southern part of the sacred space along with the paper. The southern quarter rules over our energy levels, including those needed to fight and stand firm for a just cause.

Invocation: This invocation is a little different in that it is done from the center of the space. This is really for convenience and can be adapted any way you wish.

> *From the East I call you, power of the winds.*
> *By my will and your blessing, the magick shall*
> *   begin.*
> *From the South I call you, power of the flame,*
> *Energize the magick, your strength I duly claim.*
> *From the West I call you, power of the moon.*
> *Shine with courage, light the night... pray grant this*
> *   boon.*
> *From the North I call you, power of the Earth*
> *Give to me your rooted strength, let me know*
> *   my worth!*

At this point you can add a personal prayer about your situation. When you're done, move to the southern point of the space, where the candle burns. Extend your hands toward the flame so you can sense its warmth. Take a deep breath and whisper:

> *Strength be mine,*
> *Courage shine!*

Keep repeating this chant until it naturally grows louder and reaches a pinnacle. At that point, take the paper and purposefully fold it in thirds inward (for body, mind, and spirit) focusing your will and continuing to chant. Use the candle to seal the fold by dripping wax on it. If you wish, this is a great time to etch a symbol in the wax to represent your goal. You can now use this as a portable charm to encourage fortitude.

Should you ever need a lot of strength or courage quickly, open the seal and burn the paper to release all the energy inside.

Other activities: Strength is a function of will, which is considered located around the solar plexus chakra. Sit down and visualize this as a spinning wheel of energy above your solar plexus. As you visualize, also imagine a golden-yellow light pouring down from above you, through your head, down through your heart, and into the solar plexus. Continue until clarity of light and color in the chakra is as true as possible. This activity helps cleanse and balance that chakra to provide greater willpower.

Closing: Return to the center of your circle and say:

> *Return, return, all powers return*
> *To the place from which you come;*
> *The place from which you've ever been*
> *Merry meet, merry part, and merry meet again!*

Transition Ritual

How often do we hear the phrase "times change?" These days, things change faster than most people change socks! When you find you're having trouble keeping up with transitions or adjusting to them, this candle ritual is designed to help.

What you'll need: Four candles, each of which should be one of the four elemental colors (red, blue, yellow, green). A good choice of aromatics for this ritual is lavender, as it inspires an inner peace with whatever matters face you. Alternatively try sandalwood for spiritual centering.

Setting up the space: Place the four candles at their appropriate points of the circle (red in the South, blue in the West, yellow in the East, and green in the North). Have matches or a fire source handy from which to light them during the ritual.

Also, if you can, work at dawn, dusk, noon, or midnight. These are all transitional moments of the day, and their energy is beneficial.

Invocation: This ritual is a little unique in that the invocation itself includes the magickal activity aimed at helping you adjust to energy. Pay particular attention to the instructions given at each Quarter point and focus on your intention deeply. There's no reason to rush!

Begin in the North (thinking of the circle like a clock face, this is noon). Light the candle and turn it around clockwise, as you say:

> *Turn and change, turn and change,*
> *All things turn and change.*
> *My entire life's been rearranged*
> *Yet still, I turn and change.*

Move to the East, gently whispering "turn and change" until you reach the candle. This helps carry the energy created in the North with you and connect it to the East. Light the candle and turn it clockwise, saying:

> *Change and turn, change and turn,*
> *All things change and turn.*
> *Many a lesson shall I learn,*
> *Yet still I change and turn!*

Move to the South, letting your voice grow stronger as you continue to repeat "change and turn" while walking. Stop at the red candle, light it, and turn it clockwise, saying:

> *The fires burn, the fires transform.*
> *All things, the fires transform.*
> *And in the ash, new life is born.*
> *And so I shall transform!*

Move to the West, continuing to let your voice grow in strength, this time simply repeating the word "transform." Stop at the blue candle, light it, and start turning it clockwise, saying:

Adapt and flow, adapt and flow,
Waters adapt and flow.
As above so below,
And so I adapt and flow!

Now go sit in the center of the circle and meditate for as long as you wish. The power of transformation and the ability to accept surrounds. All you need do is allow them to saturate your being.

Other activities: Many of the luck-changing activities discussed earlier in this chapter work for changing one's perspectives too. Simply alter the colors, aromatics, wording, and personal focus to suit your goal and use whichever ones you like.

Closing: Stand up in the middle of your circle and say:

Time comes and goes, but magick endures.
Guardians, I thank you for your help this day.
And like the magick,
Let your lessons endure in my heart.
So be it.

Beginning in the West, blow out the candles counterclockwise in silence.

Wisdom Ritual

I know of few people in the world who could not benefit from a little extra wisdom! Every day we are faced with decisions that could change our futures and affect everyone we love. We're faced with moral struggles that leave us wanting for answers. Rituals for wisdom help us face these ongoing moments using life's previous experiences and an innate sense of awareness as helpmates.

What you'll need: I've always considered purple to be the color of wisdom. You may disagree, and if so you, should pick three candles whose colors represent this attribute to you. Carve on each of them the image of an eye. In ancient times, this was a symbol of vision, understanding, and erudition. It also represents the window to the soul, where wisdom should lodge itself to grow outward into our reality.

Aromatics suited to this goal include peach and sage, which can be dabbed on the candles or burned as incense. Additionally, if you want to consider effective lunar timing, look to the full moon, which opens our third eye and provides insight.

Setting up the space: You can place the candles in your sacred space in one of two ways. First is simply to put them in the middle of the altar (handy and functional). Second is to put them at the elemental point best suited to the area of your life in which wisdom is needed. For example, if you need to learn how to manage money more wisely, put them in the North. If you need to be wiser in the way you express yourself, put them in the East.

Invocation: If there's a direction in which you placed the candles, begin this invocation there and follow around the circle clockwise. Otherwise, begin in the traditional point of the East (the East represents dawn and new beginnings, as that's where the sun rises), saying:

> *Ancient power of the East, I come to you.*
> *Here, between the worlds I seek your counsel.*
> *Be welcome and greet me with new ideas.*
>
> *Ancient power of the South, I come to you.*
> *Here between dawn and darkness, I seek your*
> *counsel.*
> *Be welcome and greet me with refreshed energy.*

Ancient power of the West, I come to you.
Here between the tides, I seek your counsel.
Be welcome and greet me with profound insight.

Ancient power of the North, I come to you.
Here between life and death, I seek your counsel.
Be welcome and greet me with your lessons.

Go to the area where you have set out the three candles and light one at a time, saying:

Wisdom in body: I reclaim my body as a temple in
*   which spiritual learning and growth are taking*
*   place.*
Let me treat it wisely.

Wisdom in mind: I claim my thoughts, knowing
*   thoughts are power through which change is*
*   manifest.*
Let me think clearly and wisely.

Wisdom in spirit: I claim my soul in all its
*   knowledge gained from past lives. Let those*
*   lessons reawaken*
*   and bring me wisdom.*

This is a good time to sit quietly and meditate. Spirit speaks when we are ready to listen and ritual is a means of opening ourselves to those messages.

Other activities: Bring a glass of peach-flavored juice with you into the space. After the main activity, sit in the center of the space holding it to the sky and saying something like:

In my heart, wisdom shall shine.
When I drink this juice, wisdom is mine!

As you can see, not the greatest poetry! Remember, it's the intention, not the words that count. Then drink every last drop of the juice to welcome that energy into yourself.

Closing: I suggest formalizing a prayer with your own words for the closing of this ritual, expressing to the Powers and the Sacred the reason for your need, and your willingness to be careful with what you're given. Remember: wisdom is a gift like any other and needs to be honored.

ৡৡৡ

This is just a small sampling of rituals that have candles as a focal point. What other kinds of rituals could you perform similarly? Nearly any! You can create rituals for health, wealth, happiness, fertility, and so on—in other words, candle rituals can be applied to all common needs. You can also get clever and come up with generic wish rituals. For example, get a floating candle of a suitable color and hold a ritual near a source of flowing water. Light it and make a wish during the rite, placing it gently on the water. The water's movement carries the light of your hope out to the world.

Feng Shui and Candles

6

The best and safest thing is to keep a balance in your life,
acknowledge the great powers around us and in us.
—Euripides

I n Chapter 4 we discussed the Buddhist model for candlelit prayers and meditations, in which intention is the key to manifestation. With this in mind, it is not surprising that another Eastern methodology and philosophy lends itself nicely to candle magick: feng shui. Known in modern circles as the art of placement, feng shui began in China some 4,000 years ago as a system that recognizes and honors the elements as important powers influencing our lives.

In feng shui the hope is to inspire the most positive flow of chi, which equates (for lack of a better way of saying it) to "good vibes." Chi is part of all things. It is in rocks and trees, and it is in our homes and sacred spaces. As we learn to recognize and work with chi, it promotes wealth, joy, and wholeness in body, mind, and spirit.

The next obvious question is, "What on earth does this have to do with candles?" Quite a bit when you understand it better. Each part of a room, a home, a yard, or any space in which one might enact magick has a specific type of chi associated with it. Just as we speak of Earth, Air, Fire, and Water as having unique energies that can promote specific types of magick, feng shui works similarly, focusing on placement as the key to success. And like magick, feng shui is said to be able to affect people over long distances as long as that person has lived in your home or been to your sacred space before.

Feng Shui Directions/Correspondences

In order to begin to apply the philosophy of feng shui to candle-lighting, one must first know what part of any space represents which element. In addition, we need to understand what those elements control in this specific philosophical system. Although I still encourage people to trust their instincts about symbolic value, it is also important to honor the cultural system from which we're deriving information.

Following are the rest of the directions moving clockwise around a space. As you review the directions, bear in mind that every space and every subsection of a space will house these directions. This means that your entire home can be broken up in this manner, and so could the single room in which you work your magick. This will give you more flexibility in your candle-lighting efforts.

Direction	Theme, Color, Element
North	Ability to nurture, jobs, career-oriented energy. Black and blue. Water.
Northeast	Learning, education, conscious mind. Brown and yellow. Earth.
East	Family, health, spring, beginnings, stimulation. Light blue and shoot green. Wood.
Southeast	Prosperity, abundance, inventiveness. Dark green, blue. Wood.
South	Acceptance, renown, recognition, energy. Red and purple. Fire.
Southwest	Relationships (love-oriented), joy, contentment, peace. Brown and yellow. Earth.
West	Children's fortune, harmony. White, silver, gold. Metal.
Northwest	Service, helpful people, networking. White, silver, gold. Metal.

Let's take a moment to look at these more closely.

North

North is the financial district, at least regarding career. This part of a room or house indicates how successful you are in your career, how you interact with co-workers, how content you are about your work, and the overall balance you've achieved between home and work. For example, let's say the kitchen is in this part of your house. You may be someone with a career as a chef, someone who likes to nibble on the job, or you may find that things in your career are constantly "cooking." However, if the kitchen is very dark or poorly organized, you might find your mood at work is similarly dark and your desk in a constant state of disarray. Take down the curtains, get things in order, and light a candle so a positive change can begin!

Northeast

It is very interesting to look at your home and consider what rooms or objects sit in this region. For example, if it happens to be the bathroom, you'll find that nearly everyone in your home reads in here—and not just the light stuff either! On a more serious note, developing one's mind is an important factor for spiritual success too. So pay attention to this quarter of your home or sacred space, and honor it with a candle of the appropriate color when you find your thoughts or focus wandering.

By the way, this is also a good place to light a candle when you're suffering mental distress, as it accents the rational self. Or light a candle to expand your mind in new and interesting directions.

East

This direction is just as important in feng shui as it is in magick. This is the direction of growth and new beginnings, like Spring itself. So if you're having trouble getting a project off the ground or feeling under the weather, take a look at this part of your home or room. Is it dirty? Cluttered? Does something seem amiss? Clean, straighten or fix the problem, then purposefully light a candle there to put the chi back into harmony. Watch what happens!

Southeast

At this point of the circle, we are starting to move into sun-related energy, which brings blessings. Many businesspeople in the East make sure to keep a flowering plant in the southeast section of their office or home so that prosperity similarly flowers. Note that when combined with a candle-lighting in the East, this can also get a special project off on the best possible footing.

By the way, for artists suffering from blockage, this is an ideal spot to clear out those issues and get some fresh ideas. Make sure there are no closed doors and blocked views in this area, then light a candle to get things back on track.

South

This part of a room or home has a great deal of influence over other people's perceptions of you and your efforts. It also speaks loudly of virtues such as honor, courage, and composure. Individuals who are wallflowers, who lack real enthusiasm for life, or those who feel as if everyone gossips against them would to well to examine this region. For example, if the area is very closed in, you may find that people see you as similarly closed-minded. Opening this up releases the positive chi and begins the process of re-patterning. Combined with candle-lighting, this also helps clear out residual negative memories or impressions.

Southwest

This is a part of a home or room that should never be neglected, as it rules over matters of love, luck, understanding, empathy, and unity. If you find that the overall harmony of your family seems constantly out of whack in one part of the house, open all the doors leading from the southwest area into this room so the love flows in!

This is an excellent region in which to light relationship candles aimed at straightening your present relationships and improving the overall communications in your home. You might also light a candle here when bringing a new person into your life, or even a pet. Each living being that we accept into our lives changes the energy with which we're working regularly. Candle-lighting in this feng shui sector acknowledges that shift and honors it, making the transitions easier.

West

Many people will read the phrase "children's fortune" and skip reading about the West, thinking: "I don't have any children." Well, I have a surprise for you—you probably have metaphorical children. Is there something you've created from scratch of which you're terribly proud (art or a business)? Is there an animal in your life that you treat like a baby? Or is there a child—a niece, nephew, grandchild, or friend's child— with whom you have a very strong connection? If so, working candle magick in this region helps any of these "children" when health is ailing, to improve behavior, or just to bring a lifetime filled with joy.

Northwest

This part of the sacred space resonates with the energy of service freely given. Frequently this comes from others to you, but it can also be quite indicative of how graciously you're able to give of yourself. If you find that you're hesitant to contribute in healthy ways to the lives of others, the chi here is very likely blocked. Put things in order, get rid of the clutter, open a window, and open yourself. Light a candle to represent a perceptive spirit, ready to give and receive.

Working in this area helps us during those times when we need other people to move and shake things, or just to support us during difficult times. In this case, lighting the candle acts like an invitation for the chi to reach out and touch those whose presence, knowledge, or aid will be most beneficial.

By the way, for those of you who work with ancestral spirits, this is the ideal place to honor them. Our ancestors are the "helpful people" who forged our reality as we know it. This is also an ideal location in which to enact candle spells and rituals for expanding your network of like-minded people.

Energy Levels and Directions

Just as each feng shui direction has specific associations, each also bears an energy signature. The vibrancy or quietness of this signature will often affect your candlelight rituals and spells. So here is an overview of the energy levels for your reference and ideas on how to apply them:

North

Like the Earth itself, North is very nurturing. This direction helps sustain life, so it's suited to candle magick aimed at protecting children, improving health, and giving lagging motivation a kick-start.

Northeast

This quarter houses the energy of abundance and growth. Mind you, nothing happens quickly here; Nature's way is not always speedy. Additionally, for the abundance to come to you, this quarter makes you work for it. You are a co-creator, and that means putting forth effort. Consequently any time you're learning a new skill or making concrete efforts to have magick manifest in reality, light a candle here.

East

East is where all things begin, and it is filled with vigorous energy. Procrastinators will find working candle magick in this quarter very helpful. Additionally, if there's a lot of red tape binding up a project, light a candle here to stimulate some activity.

Southeast

This is a very gentle quarter that also has some energy aimed at consistent, measured progress. This is not a flash and fanfare region, nor is it an area to work for fast results. Rather, this energy emphasizes building slowly and carefully. Artists would do well to light a candle here to shape their vision into something that will endure for a long time.

South

Like Fire itself, this energy is very vibrant. And, like fire, this energy can warm and motivate or burn and destroy, so use it very carefully. If your energy is lagging, or tenacity seems wanting, light a candle here to put a fire under your spirit.

Southwest

We find comfort in this direction. If you're having trouble de-stressing or sleeping, this is an excellent spot in which to enact candle meditations with a relaxing theme.

West

This direction brings composure and serenity. When the world seems to bombard you with troubles or tension, and the house is in complete disarray, light a candle here to restore harmony.

Northwest

The energy in this part of a room or home stretches your magick to new heights. Positive energy blossoms from here, but so can negativity, so be careful of your thoughts and actions while working in this area. In particular, if you're having trouble getting your point across, or if people are misinterpreting your intentions, light a candle here and all will become clear.

Applying Feng Shui Color Correspondences to Candle-Lighting

Every culture has slightly different ways of looking at color. Because feng shui is as much a philosophy as it is an art, it too has specific ideas about what colors represent. If you're working with the feng shui quarters, it makes sense to maintain congruity by using the right representative colors as provided by this system. Here's an overview for your reference:

Black: Deeper mysteries, intense clarity, knowing one's limits, karma, personal growth. Most effective in the center point of a space.

Blue: Gentility, creativity, balance, happiness, beauty, giving freely, literal or figurative wealth. Most effective in the North.

Gold: Wealth, vitality, the ancient wisdom and power of the dragon. Most effective in the South.

Green: Business, decision making, tenacity, prosperity, order, progress, harmony, wellness, good advice. Most effective in the East.

Indigo: Truth, honesty, Ancestral energy, foreknowledge, exploration, knowledge's continuance (tradition), discipline. Most effective in the Northeast.

Orange: Tenderness, sagacity, time, honor, dependability, coherence, protection, overcoming fear and confusion, willpower. Most effective in the Southeast.

Purple: Leadership, spirituality, humility, generosity, peace, fulfillment, abundance, knowing the Sacred. Most effective in the Northwest.

Red: Adventure, passion, shrewdness, happiness, long-term relationships, kindness, activity. Most effective in the South.

Pink: Similar energies to red, but gentler, tactful, and subtle. Use in the South for greatest success.

Yellow: Maturity, knowledge, wishes, security, caution, mental keenness, protection from spirits, achievement, companionship. Most effective in the Southwest.

White: Overcoming barriers, becoming one with All, cycles, soul memory, personal chi, children, travel. Most effective in the West.

Applying Elemental Correspondences to Candle-Lighting

Another way to enhance chi when you're lighting candles is to bring more of a specific region's element into it. For example, we know that the East and Southeast are wood—but what if that the southeastern part of your home is filled with plastic? You may find yourself overly dependent on credit cards. Replace some of the plastic with natural wood and then light a candle to honor the chi and get rid of those mounting interest rates. The traditional color for wood is green.

Just to recap: Fire resides in the southern part of a home or room. So if this part of the house isn't getting enough light, you may likewise find that your efforts don't get much attention from others. Lighting a candle here is the perfect way of combining the element with the quarter. Traditional colors to use here include red and purple.

Water resides in the northern part of a home or room. When you notice your career seems to be stagnating, that's the time to put more water in this section (like a fish tank or a water cooler). You can certainly add candle-lighting to this effort, but keep the candles small so the Fire energy doesn't turn all the water to steam. Use the colors of blue or black.

Metal's directions are West and Northwest. When there isn't enough of that element in the West, your children may be ill or having troubles. When lacking in the Northwest, you may find it nearly impossible to get any kind of help with a pressing project. One good way to bring this element into those spaces and effectively combine it with candle-lighting is to get metal candle holders. The best wax colors to use for metal are white, silver, and gold.

Finally, Earth resides in the Southwest and Northeast. Too little Earth in the Southwest results in relationship roller coasters, a lack of self-love, or sadness. In the Northeast, it results in difficulty in applying yourself to new tasks, poor con-centration, or learning problems. Offset this by taking a nice container of rich potting soil with a candle secured in the middle (this makes a fire-safe container), and igniting the candle to get the energy back on track. Traditional Earth colors are brown, yellow, and tan.

Now, I should note that too much of an element can also prove problematic. For example:

- **Fire:** Too much Fire in the South leads to an un-healthy focus on achievement and the need for rec-ognition, or possibly receiving unwanted attentions. Too much Fire in the Southwest creates a relation-ship based on passion over love, or potentially one filled with anger. Spiritually, a person surrounded by too much Fire will have a tendency to burn out.

- **Water:** Too much Water literally floods things out. When there's too much in the North, your career might seem muddy. When there's too much in the East, people in your home might suffer from sniffles frequently. Spiritually, too much of the

Water element makes one wishy-washy and a little too easily influenced by others.

- **Wood:** Wood represents health, family, and wealth. When it's out of balance you could find yourself with visiting in-laws who never want to leave, prosperity that's fleeting, or odd swings in physical health. On the other hand, a lot of Wood in the Northeast section could lead to a fairly successful career focus in the fields of health education or financial counseling. Spiritually, too much could lead to an inner struggle between family responsibilities and personal spiritual needs. Too little Wood, on the other hand, tends to leave a person spiritually impoverished because his or her focus is often in the wrong place.

- **Metal:** Too much Metal in the North can lead to buying tons of jewelry or metallic items (rather than saving the money for other things). Since Metal's directions are West and Northwest, too much can bring a desire for more children than one can financially support, or a person who collects relationships like some people collect coins. Spiritually speaking, too much Metal can lead to materialistic spirituality, whereas too little could inspire overspending on magickal trinkets that really aren't necessary to one's growth and maturity.

- **Earth:** Earth is an element associated with the conscious mind (learning) and relationships. Too much Earth often results in the perpetual student syndrome or a tendency to be very clingy because the need for security in relationships seems overwhelming. Spiritually, when there's too much Earth we can find ourselves being too focused on logic and the concrete world and unable to touch Spirit.

Bear in mind that the elements can provide you with a little more flexibility in your candle-lighting work. For example, to bring more passion (Fire) into a relationship, you might want to light more red or purple candles in the Southwest. Or, to give that relationship more solid foundations, light brown or yellow candles here to bring Earth into the equation.

Timing for Feng Shui Candle-Lighting

As in magickal traditions, feng shui regards every hour of every day as supporting a specific type of chi. So if you want to augment your candle-lighting efforts in specific quarters by timing them according to this tradition, you can follow this list:

Fire (South): 12 p.m. to 3 p.m.
Earth (Southwest): 3 p.m. to 6 p.m.
Metal (West): 6 p.m. to 9 p.m.
Metal (Northwest): 9 p.m. to 12 a.m.
Earth (North): 12 a.m. to 3 a.m.
Earth (Northeast): 3 a.m. to 6 a.m.
Wood (East): 6 a.m. to 9 a.m.
Wood (Southeast): 9 a.m. to 12 p.m.

By the way, at the point of transition (6 p.m., for example), two elements are both active at the same time, so you get the combination of their energies. If you're looking for the purest elemental energy, go for the halfway point of the three-hour period for that element. For example, Wood for the eastern quarter is most likely to be fully active and clear right around 7:30 a.m.

Putting this all together in a specific example, let's say you wanted to get recognition for a task at work that everyone seems to completely overlook. This corresponds to the southern point of a room or home. So, take a red candle to this point and light it between the hours of 12 noon and 3 p.m., adding whatever other elements you desire to this action (like an incantation, carvings, or aromatics). Note that if you light a candle at the beginning of an elemental period, it strengthens the effect to leave it to burn the entire three hours (as three is the number of body, mind, and spirit).

Mirrors and Feng Shui

Mirrors are frequently used in feng shui to redirect energy where it needs to go. Let's face it, not all of us can build or remodel a house to the best possible energy specifications. So if you've been suffering from financial trouble and the money center of your home happens to be the bathroom, putting a mirror above the toilet helps override the negative implications of "flushing away" your prosperity.

Similarly, when negativity seems to be coming into your home from external sources, it's not uncommon to place a mirror in a window facing outward and light a candle there. Both turn away unwanted influences. The only place where it's not considered good to have mirrors is in the bedroom facing you as you sleep. According to tradition, this can make you ill and deplete your resources.

Physical Manifestations of Unbalanced Chi

Whereas Western medicine has a tendency to separate the body and spirit of a person, Eastern ideals regard them as a whole, functioning unit. This is also true in magickal traditions. So, when the chi in a person's life is out of whack, he or she may very likely suffer physical manifestations of that imbalance.

Here is a brief overview of the kinds of maladies that often develop when the chi of one's home or room isn't quite right:

North: Asthma, blood disease, cancer, digestion problems, ear infection, hearing loss, heartburn, hiccups, reproductive problems, toothaches or unusual decay, ulcers.

Northeast: Abscesses, bronchitis, constipation, finger problems, laryngitis, obesity, hemorrhoids, tonsils, nodes on the vocal cords.

South: Bone problems, easy bruising, colds, depression, eye trouble, lifeless and breakable hair, anxiety attacks, knee troubles, skin rashes, yeast infections.

Southwest: Burping, sour stomach, bladder infections, constipation, kidney problems, menstrual irregularity, pelvic problems, nasal problems.

East: Thinning hair, pimples, swelling in the joints, dizziness, earache, foot problems, fever, migraine, cold sores, nosebleeds, canker sores, tooth problems.

Southeast: Leg and ankle problems, water retention, colds, allergies, sprains, swelling.

West: Lower back pain, balance or perspective problems, bloodsugar problems, fertility, varicose veins, blood disorders.

Northwest: Fever, balding, pink eye, fainting, forearm trouble, headache, over-susceptibility to heat, breathing problems, spinal problems, wrist problems.

How do you use this information? Well, say that you've had an ongoing ache in your lower back but can't think of anything specific you've done to aggravate it. Check the western quarter of your room or home (especially the room in which you spend the most time) and see what's there. Ask yourself:

- Is there enough metal in that area?
- If there's a chair in that region, is it properly supportive of the lower back?
- Do you perhaps need to wear some metal (like jewelry) for a while to balance out energy?

  ∽ Do you need to light a gold or silver candle here to get the energy moving in the right direction again?

Also, don't forget to keep this region orderly. Disorder disrupts chi. This doesn't mean your room or house has to always look like a picture out of a home magazine. It just means you should make a conscious effort to keep things placed in such a way that the chi can flow freely.

A word of precaution: Under no circumstances should these concepts replace medical attention. If you have a problem, by all means see your doctor. Then use feng shui candle-lighting as a helpmate to wholeness while following your physician's instructions.

Neutral Territory

Thus far we haven't looked too much at the center of this giant circle we've created out of the directions in a room or home. Try to visualize, for a moment, what a room would look like if you set up appropriately colored feng shui candles at each of the eight directions. This creates a sacred space, just as invoking the Quarters does by your intention.

The central point of the space is neutral ground where all the powers and energies can mix and mingle freely. It is the center point of a magickal light mandala you're creating. Thus, at least for feng-shui-oriented activities, I advise placing your altar or a tool table at the central point.

Additionally, this point lends itself to some very specific functions. For example, when you need balance and symmetry, this is the place to work your magick. When equality is out of whack in a relationship, or when you truly need a neutral ground on which to work out a problem, again, return to center. In this place, beyond time and space, you can start getting to the "point" of existence, and also simply *be*.

What to Expect

Feng shui is a gentle form of transformation. A lifetime of living out of harmony with the chi will not be fixed overnight. Lighting candles and being more aware of the elements in your space will certainly put you on the path toward happier, healthier, and more spiritually centered living, but don't expect instant or overly flashy results. That is simply not the way this system works.

Also, remember that feng shui is as much an internal process as it is an external activity. Our spirit is an environment, just like a room is an environment. If you're not willing to figuratively light the candle within, the external efforts will be pretty futile. Take time to look at your heart and get rid of the clutter there too. Just like clutter in a room disrupts the flow of chi, cluttered hearts and spirits cannot accept and readily direct that flow.

Balance is the key—balance and pacing, letting gradual change happen within and without. That said, even the results of gradual change can be quite astounding. You may find that a home that was once filled with tension settles down to a sense of calm, or that you yourself are less agitated with life. The purposeful act of choosing a candle, bringing it into an area, and lighting it has done far more than add a little illumination. It has altered your thoughts, which in turn change auric energy. It is magick!

7
Astrological Candles

*Ideals are like stars: You will not succeed in touching them with your
hands, but like the seafaring man on the ocean desert of waters, you
choose them as your guides, and following them, you reach your destiny.*
—Carl Schurz

Anyone who has ever read a horoscope in the paper has had some exposure to astrology. Historical evidence indicates that this type of natural omen reading originated somewhere around 2,000 B.C. in the region of Babylon. However, it took nearly 2,000 years to refine the art to where the sky was divided into 12 parts (the zodiac) and begin to use it extensively throughout the known world as a heavenly map and predictive device.

Astrology is a very complex art that bases its predictions on the moment of a person's birth as compared with celestial bodies during that time frame. By looking at where each planet sits in a person's chart, astrologers are said to be able to ascertain one's character, tendencies, best career paths, and even a bit of what the future holds. Consequently, what we see of astrology in the form of generic horoscopes is over-generalized at best.

For the purpose of this book I'd like to look at combining astrology and candle magick from three perspectives. First is using candles according to someone's birth sign. Second is enacting candle-burning magick during specific moon signs. Third is combining candle magick with the symbolic value of other celestial objects and events. I feel these are the most common elements added to magick, and the most easily applied without needing to gather a great deal of astrological information or calculations.

Birth Signs

What's your sign? This question has become a standing joke as an old, and rather unsuccessful, pick-up line. But astrology isn't a joke for many people. Some use it to chart entire days, weeks, and even years to try to work with the energy of the universe more effectively.

If you're not familiar with the energy associated with specific signs, this will help:

Astrological Birth Sign Correspondences

Aries: The spirit of adventure, firmness, self-awareness.

Taurus: Diligence, determination, devotion, awareness of one's blessings.

Gemini: Thoughtfulness (pondering), sociability, awareness of diversity.

Cancer: Inventiveness, hearth energy, dedication, awareness of the emotional nature.

Leo: Charisma, bravery, ardor, awareness of the power of will.

Virgo: The conscious mind, logic, accountability, awareness of the value of analysis.

Libra: Peace, symmetry, beauty, manners, awareness of balance in all things.

Scorpio: Creativity, competitive spirit, profound feelings, awareness of how to wield wishcraft.

Sagittarius: Free thinking, extroversion, awareness of awakening visions.

Capricorn: Fidelity, sensibility, moderation, gentility, an awareness of how to use anything effectively.

Aquarius: Originality, optimism, enthusiasm, an awareness of knowledge's power.

Pisces: Adaptability, benevolence, empathy, instinct, an awareness of the transforming nature of faith.

I've always loved the fact that horoscope means "time observer." This is a very accurate description, especially because what we're doing is watching the time of a person's birth to determine the best color candle to use in our magick. There is only one problem with this idea. During my research I discovered that various cultures and individuals have interpreted the colors of the zodiac differently! This left me with the difficult task of deciding what information to pass along to you as a reference point.

In order to facilitate things a bit, I decided to list the most commonly noted astrological colors (in other words, the ones that appeared in more than one correspondence list for a specific sign). From here, you must let the theme of the magick and your instincts guide you in the actual decision-making process.

Astrological Colors

Note: In listing the colors, I put the hue that showed up most predominantly in my research first, with secondary colors following.

Aries (March 21 to April 19): Red, pink.

Taurus (April 20 to May 21): Green, yellow, pink, pale blue.

Gemini (May 22 to June 21): Yellow, violet, red.

Cancer (June 22 to July 22): Pastels, silver, gray, green.

Leo (July 23 to August 23): Gold, orange, red, green.

Virgo (August 24 to September 23): Blue, gray, green, violet, gold, yellow.

Libra (September 24 to October 23): Rose, blue, yellow, pale green, pale blue.

Scorpio (October 24 to November 22): Red, black, maroon, brown.

Sagittarius (November 23 to December 21): Purple, midnight blue, gold, red.

Capricorn (December 22 to January 20): Brown, dark blue, dark green, red.

Aquarius (January 21to February 19): Bright blue, indigo, lavender, green.

Pisces (February 20 to March 20): Green, turquoise, pale violet, white, mauve.

The next obvious question is how to apply this knowledge to candle magick. Here are several ideas:

- During any candle-burning technique, have at least one candle colored with a supportive astrological hue for your birth sign (this can represent you in the working).

- Light a candle of the appropriate color on your birthday, which then accents all the best attributes of your birth sign in you.

- When doing candle magick for someone else, choose a candle whose color fits his or her birth sign.

༯ When you need specific qualities that are part of other astrological signs, choose candles whose colors can represent those signs and use them in your working.

༯ Meditate with a candle whose color represents your sign when trying to activate that sign's best qualities in and around your life.

༯ Choose a birth candle whose color also has symbolic value to a spell or ritual. For example, if your birth sign is Pisces, you might choose a pale purple candle when working on matters of spiritual growth, or a green candle for prosperity.

༯ Finally, light an appropriate colored candle to honor the arrival of new birth signs throughout the year. Symbolically this represents the movement of all things both on Earth and in the larger universe. By the way, if you can keep pillar candles set up in a circle (like the face of a clock) for this purpose, it makes a really beautiful accent to an altar or other sacred space. Better still, because you reuse these candles annually, their positive energy continues to grow!

Combining Astrology, Candles, and Aromatics

Our senses help give greater dimension to our magick. So, adding the correct aromatic associations to your candles (dressing with oil), the room (via incense), or even yourself (cologne, perfume, or whatever) for magickal processes makes a lot of sense.

Here is a chart of some of the scents whose energies support those of specific birth signs:

Astrological Aromatics

Aries: Cinnamon, clove, pine, musk.

Taurus: Apple, lilac, thyme, rose, vanilla.

Gemini: Dill, almond, mint.

Cancer: Eucalyptus, jasmine, lemon, sandalwood.

Leo: Laurel, angelica, sage, frankincense.

Virgo: Cedar, lavender, orange, rosemary.

Libra: Geranium, bergamot, primrose, thyme.

Scorpio: Basil, patchouli, allspice, violet.

Sagittarius: Cedar, ginger, orange.

Capricorn: Patchouli, vetivert, honeysuckle.

Aquarius: Anise, almond, lavender, pine, mint.

Pisces: Passion flower, nutmeg, lemon, jasmine.

Putting aromatics together with your candle magick is really pretty easy. You can:

- Dress the colored astrological candle with an aromatic that supports that sign.
- Dress the colored astrological candle with an aromatic that represents another sign to blend the associated energy.
- Dress a white candle with an astrological aromatic when you don't have a candle of the right color.
- Dress a white candle with an astrological aromatic to represent a person or situation to whom the energy is being directed.
- Burn incense in place of dressing the candle (or as an additional aromatic support)
- Wear or bathe in oils of an appropriate scent so you carry that energy in your aura into the working.

ॐ Dab the lightbulbs in your home with the
appropriate aromatic to turn on that energy
when you need it most. Note that a lightbulb is
the modern version of a candle.

Finally, consider putting incense on a windowsill or dab
the window ledge with oils. Sunlight is another kind of fire
that can activate your energy when a candle isn't available or
safe to use.

Combining Astrology, Candles, and Crystals

In Chapter 1 we talked a bit about making candles that
have crystals in the base, powdered crystals in the wax, or that
are decorated on the outside with crystals. Here's another opportunity to put that idea to work. This time, make your astrological candles with a crystal that provides extra energy for
whatever purpose you have in mind. Use the following guide:

Astrological Rock and Metal Correspondences

Aries: Ruby, red jasper, carnelian, coral, diamond, bloodstone,
garnet, gold, bronze.

Taurus: Emerald, golden topaz, lapis, jade, azurite, agate, silver, gold, copper.

Gemini: Crystal, aquamarine, alexandrite, beryl, pearl, agate,
aventurine, gold, silver.

Cancer: Ruby, moonstone, pearl, green turquoise, silver, beryl.

Leo: Amber, sardonyx, ruby, jacinth, peridot, carnelian, topaz,
gold.

Virgo: Pink jasper, rhodochrosite, azurite, sapphire, star sapphire, aventurine, gold.

Libra: Opal, fire agate, agate, tourmaline, lapis, turquoise.

Scorpio: Topaz, garnet, coral, ruby, zircon, gold, kunzite, silver.

Sagittarius: Amethyst, malachite, zircon, turquoise, silver, sugilite, gold, copper.

Capricorn: Onyx, quartz, beryl, jet, garnet, obsidian, hematite, gold, silver.

Aquarius: Blue sapphire, lapis, aquamarine, amethyst, jet.

Pisces: Diamond, turquoise, jade, tourmaline, bloodstone, amethyst, sugilite, silver.

Use this information similarly to what's been described for the aromatics and colors. For example, if you're an Aquarius and you want to make a candle to accent the best characteristics of that sign, you'd probably cast it out of lavender wax (scented with lavender) and decorate it with an amethyst or lapis. Another example would be an Aries making a red candle scented with cinnamon and decorated with a bloodstone. In both examples here, note the harmony between the three component choices (wax color, aromatic, crystal) and their traditional magickal associations.

If for some reason you'd rather not put crystals in the wax, you can simply place the stone on your altar with the candle and then carry it afterward to keep the magick with you. Another alternative is finding candle holders that have appropriate crystals inlaid in them to create a base of positive vibrations from which the candle can burn.

Magick in the Moon

There is an old saying that witches get power from the moon. There were many reasons for this belief, not the least of which was that the ancient Goddess was often associated with the moon. So it's not surprising to discover that as the moon moves through the signs of the zodiac it is said to have a specific influence on the energies of that sign.

To effectively use the information I'm about to share, you'll need a good astrological calendar that lists the moon signs. That way you can time your magickal efforts to a moon sign that best suits your goals. Although it is certainly not necessary to do this all the time, you can think of celestial influences as another support system for your magick. When the moon is in the right place for the right job, it aids manifestation (there are more timing ideas in Chapter 1).

Moon in Aries:	Purification, overcoming obstacles, developing skills or talents, leadership, bravery.
Moon in Taurus:	Resourcefulness, efficiency, fortitude, relief or comfort, the muse, glamoury, rational thinking.
Moon in Gemini:	Adjustment, overcoming bad habits or negative thought forms, transformation, adaptability.
Moon in Cancer:	Inventiveness, abundance, moon magick, sensitivity, romance, water magick.
Moon in Leo:	Learning (especially a skill), developing personal characteristics, loyalty, courage, honor.
Moon in Virgo:	Fertility, prosperity, success, inner sense of peace, practicality.
Moon in Libra:	Symmetry, insight, truthfulness, justice, decision-making.
Moon in Scorpio:	Energy, passion, sexual ability and appeal, turning negative energy, charisma, emotional openness.
Moon in Sagittarius:	Grounding, moderation, self-mastery, goal-oriented magick, honesty, willpower, frankness, tolerance, equality, optimism.

Moon in Capricorn: Rooting out secrets or hidden matters, ingathering, spiritual development, patience, persistence.

Moon in Aquarius: Idealism, charity, empathy, kindness, inspiration, joy, adventure, socialization.

Moon in Pisces: Action, progress, developing or listening to instinct, creativity, psychism, compassion, romance.

Don't forget that you can easily combine this knowledge with a specifically colored, dressed, or decorated candle to further the energy. For example, if working magick for self-mastery when the moon is in Sagittarius, it makes sense to use a purple candle (good for introspection), ginger oil (for energy), and a copper candle holder. All three of these things also happen to be associated with the sign of Sagittarius. Another example would be to use a rose-colored candle (for self-love), dabbed with bergamot (success) and decorated with a turquoise (safety) to reestablish inner harmony when the moon is in Virgo.

As you can see from these examples, I'm not only using the astrological symbolism of the additional elements to help the magick along. I'm also using their traditional metaphysical associations, and they all work together marvelously. This is just one more way to add a personal touch to your magick.

Other Celestial Helpers

The moon is certainly not alone in the night sky, and consequently many magickal beliefs were ascribed to other celestial objects and phenomena. I present these here for your consideration for those times when you feel your magick might need a little extra oomph!

Aurora Borealis:

In northern climates, the appearance of the Northern Lights often portends good luck or heroic enterprises. If you should happen to glimpse them one night, light a candle for improved fortune or fame.

Constellations:

The constellations were like huge storybooks in the sky for our ancestors, and as we know, many of them became the foundation for our astrological systems today. When a constellation you recognize is in the heavens, and it has specific meaning to you, honor that moment with a candle and a spell or two. For example, you might work candle magick for success and victory when Hercules is predominant in the night sky, or work magick for honor and a higher perspective when Aquilla (the eagle) appears. Watch your local newspapers for star charts that can act as a guide for where to look in the night sky for these and other symbolic constellations.

Eclipse:

A magickal practitioner could not wish for a better symbol of the in-between place—between thought and action, between sound and silence, and most importantly between the worlds. Light a candle during an eclipse to bring greater balance in your life, or when you need help adjusting to important changes.

Falling Stars (comets and meteors):

Traditionally these are wished upon. Beyond this, falling stars and comets were often regarded as heralds of important events. When you see one, light a candle and whisper your wish to the universe. Or, light a candle and ask Spirit what you should be paying more attention to. Remember to listen for an answer!

Planets:

Some planets we can see with the naked eye, particularly Venus. Even those we cannot see, however, are said to have an influence on our lives. In particular, every bit of greenery on our planet has pretty well been categorized as being ruled by one of the planets in both ancient and modern systems. This ruling energy, in turn, affects the plant's spiritual attributes.

What does all this mean for candle magick? Well if the newspaper's star chart shows a planet hovering in your region of the night sky, light a candle to honor its influence and energy (especially if it's energy you need). Here's an overview of each planet's characteristics:

Mercury: Communication, learning, trade, business, teaching, public impressions.

Mars: The warrior spirit, aggression, victory.

Jupiter: Health and healing, integrity, protocol.

Saturn: Meditation, thoughtfulness, introspection, focus.

Venus: Relationships (especially love), success, creativity, the muse, spontaneity.

(Note: the reason the rest of the planets are not included here is because they hadn't been discovered at the time when classifications began.)

Sun:

We often overlook the sun because we see it daily and it doesn't seem to change. Thanks to science, however, we know that the sun is full of ever-transforming energy, and that power is the key word for this celestial object. In particular the sun represents the God aspect, leadership qualities, logic, nobility, wisdom, independence, comprehension, strength, and victory. Lighting candles on days like the Summer Solstice, or at times like noon when the sun is strong, accents those characteristics.

Also, as I mentioned briefly earlier this chapter, the sun's fire can become a substitute for a candle during daylight hours. After all, candles were invented to be substitute suns at night, so turnabout is fair play!

ço·ço·ço

Although I know that not everyone will be able to time candle magick to the signs, or use every bit of symbolic value the signs offer, it is nice to have the information available. It gives you more flexibility and also makes us aware that there is little on Earth or in the heavens that cannot be used for magick if we understand it and honor it.

Holidays, Festivals, Gods, and Goddesses

If you have knowledge, let others light their candles at it.
—Margaret Fuller

No book on magick is wholly complete without something about holidays, observances, and the many faces of Spirit that neo-pagans revere. Magick is a joyful tradition that has many festivals. These festivals commemorate a variety of things—the seasons, important moments in our lives, world events, gods and goddesses, and so forth. But sometimes the most important part of an observance is not the theme, but rather the fact that we are taking time out to remember who we are and where we have come from, and to think a bit about where we are going as spiritual seekers.

Similarly, lighting candles for gods and goddesses or simply for Spirit has value because it acts as both an acknowledgment and an invitation. When we light a candle we say "I believe." When we light a candle, we open an inner door through which Spirit can speak to, and interact with, us every moment of every day.

Holidays, Festivals, and Observances

Holidays represent important parts of everyday life—the date of our birth, an anniversary, wise people who touch us, and so forth. Considering how important candles have been in religion and everyday life, it's not surprising to discover them participating in both kinds of holidays for thousands of years. The lighting of candles at these events represented something—a memorial or celebration, a way to honor our humanness, and a way to express our connection with the Sacred.

By learning what holidays used candles extensively and why, you can then apply that knowledge to your own magick. How? By timing your candle lighting efforts according to a specific holiday whose theme supports your magick!

Candle-Oriented Festivals

- **Carnival (early January):** Throughout Europe this was a time to have fun before restrictions of Lent set in. People traditionally carried candles while making overtures to other individuals they found attractive!

- **Candlemas (February 2):** A time in some magickal traditions for initiation rights, Candlemas is a way of giving strength to the sun when darkness still surrounds. It also reminds us that the spirit within always burns brightly. Consequently the altar is traditionally covered with an array of candles, as is the circle.

- **Valentine's Day (February 14):** This celebration goes back to ancient Roman fertility festivals. Today we continue to honor the spirit of love, often with romantic, candlelit dinners.

❧ **Festival of Vesta (March 2):** A Roman celebration of the goddess who protects sacred fires. Starting a new house candle this day is perfectly appropriate to the occasion.

❧ **Feast of the Moon Goddess (March 31):** Another Roman festival. Light 13 candles today to honor each of the 13 full moons in a year, and to bring light and fullness into your life.

❧ **Boat Festival (early April):** A French holiday during which people launch tiny boats on a river with candles and a wish. Anyone who finds one of these after the festival is guaranteed good luck!

❧ **Birthday of Buddha (April 8):** A holiday to honor this teacher. Light eight candles to remember and integrate the eight-fold path to enlightenment.

❧ **Festival of Ishtar (April 22):** This goddess of love, life, and light in Babylon is suitably honored this day by lighting candles and enjoying a little unbridled passion.

❧ **Beltane (May 1):** Also known as May Day, this is a time when we celebrate our own fertility and that of the Earth. Traditionally Beltane is a fire festival, complete with bonfires, but if you cannot have such a blaze, light some candles.

❧ **Bon Dea (May 3):** A Roman celebration of bountiful blessings. Jump a candle today for luck and purification.

❧ **Three Maries of the Sea (late May):** A French festival celebrated by gypsies that honors the three faces of the Goddess with dance, divination, song, and candlelight.

❧ **Birthday of the Muses (June 14):** A Greek celebration that we can commemorate by lighting nine candles, one for each muse (epic songs, history, lyrical songs, comedy, tragedy, dance, erotic poetry, sacred music, and astronomy). Or, just light one candle for the muse you most wish to bring into your life.

ᔐ **Summer Solstice (June 21):** Light a floating candle just before dawn and put it out on a river, lake, or ocean with a wish, then let the light of summer give that wish power.

ᔐ **Good Luck Day (June 24):** Light three candles today, one for each of the three fates, and pray for improved fortune.

ᔐ **Birthday of Isis (August 15):** The Egyptian goddess Isis is one of the most complete divine figures in all of the world's history. Lighting a candle today is said to bless one's travels, especially by boat.

ᔐ **Ilmatar's Feast (August 26):** This Finnish goddess created the world. Honor her by lighting six golden candles carved with egg images to bring her inventiveness into your life.

ᔐ **Fire Lighting Festival (September 15):** An Egyptian holiday, this is a time to light every fire source, including candles, to honor the Divine and the Ancestor spirits.

ᔐ **Durga Puja (September 25):** An Indian festival for the goddess who protects those we love. Honor her with a yellow candle.

ᔐ **Halloween (October 31):** Candles placed in pumpkins mark this holiday as a way of scaring off mischievous spirits and giving light to the night. In Mexico, people adorn their windows and sidewalks with candles to welcome the spirits of children into the home on this day, when the thin veil between worlds allows for a visit.

ᔐ **Loy Krathong (November 9):** A Thai holiday during which candles are lit on banana leaf boats and sent down river with wishes. If the candle stays lit until the boat moves out of site, the wish is said to come true.

ᔐ **Hecate's Festival (November 16):** A time to honor the patroness of witches, this festival comes from Greece. Light a candle at a crossroad to commemorate the day.

ও **Diwali (November 16):** This festival comes from India and it honors Lakshmi, a wealth goddess. Her way into the home is always lit with candles, especially ones that are gold-toned.

ও **Lucy's Day (December 13):** A holiday in Sweden, during which the eldest daughter of a house wears a crown of candles to honor the goddess of the sun, Lucina.

ও **Winter Solstice (December 21):** A festival of lights around the world. It used to be that pagans put candles in trees, along with other gifts, to give strength to nature spirits, whose energy was low at this time of year due to longer nights and the cold.

This is but a small sampling of the world's rich assembly of festivals and holidays. There are literally thousands more, many of which use candles to light the way for a better tomorrow.

Light of the God/Goddess

Nearly every civilization around the world has had a goddess who was represented by light: light in the darkness, the light that banishes shadows, the light of the world. This has a lot to do with the sun, and the fact that life for the ancients was far safer during daylight hours. The power of the symbolism of light has remained with us. Additionally, not only is the divine represented by this warm, powerful glow, but so is the human soul. This reminds us that a spark of our being is also divine, just as any child houses part of his or her parents' genetic code within.

In the context of this book, candles can be used in connection with gods and goddesses in various ways. First, we already discussed the use of a plain white candle as a generic representation of Divine presence in your rituals and spellwork. But this idea has great potential to be further refined and personalized. In particular, you can honor a god or goddess in your sacred space by using a specifically scented, colored, or carved candle.

Here is a list of deities from around the world and some of the aromatics, colors, or easily carved symbols with which they're associated:

God and Goddess Color, Aromatic, or Symbolic Associations

෨ **Aegir** (Germany): A sea god who brings tranquil winds. His color is gold. Use watery aromatics like lemon to honor him.

෨ **Agni** (Hindu): Fire god whose colors are gold or red. His symbols include an eagle. Use a wooden candle stand and put out your candle with water to honor him.

෨ **Amitabha** (Chinese): God of heaven and light who abides in the West. His sacred color is red, and his traditional symbolic representation is a lotus or a small bowl. Lotus is also a suitable aromatic to burn to honor this god.

෨ **Amun Ra** (Egyptian): Sun god whose color is gold. His aromatics include musk and cedar, and preparing a candle with turquoise or amethyst decorations can help honor him.

෨ **Aphrodite** (Greek): Goddess of passion and sex. Use a copper-colored candle dabbed with rose oil to honor her.

෨ **Apollo** (Greek, Roman): God of light, truth, creativity, and communication. A bow is a suitable symbol for him, and aromatics include cinnamon and bay.

෨ **Baldur** (Scandinavian): God of wisdom and kindness. His color is yellow or gold, and his symbol is that of the zodiac sign of Gemini.

෨ **Brahma** (Hindu): A creative and artistic force, Brahma's color is yellow or saffron. His symbols include a wheel (or circle), and a suitable dressing oil for the candles would be cedar.

- **Brighid** (Irish): Goddess of forests, fertility, and inspiration. Her colors are white and gold.

- **Callisto** (Greek): Goddess of the moon, represented by a silver candle carved with the image of a wheel.

- **Cerridwen** (Welsh): Goddess of inspiration and providence, she is typically represented by dark colors and a cauldron.

- **Chandra** (Hindu): God of the moon, whose color is silver or white. Use almond or aloe to anoint your candles, and do so in full moonlight to honor him.

- **Cupid** (Roman): God of love, who can be suitably represented by a passionate color of red or a bow and arrow.

- **Dharma** (Hindu): Spirit of the law and conduct, whose color is blue and whose symbol is a club.

- **Dionysus** (Greek, Thracian): God of forests and fertility. Dab his candles with wine or carve them with the image of horns.

- **Diana** (Roman): Goddess of nature and the moon. Her color is white, a suitable aromatic for her is almond, and her symbols include a bow and arrow.

- **Dolma** (Tibetan, Nepalese, Mongolian): The goddess who embodies the best of all traits, both wise and sensuous. Her color is white, her aroma is lotus, and she can be represented by a simple star.

- **Ea** (Babylonian): God of wisdom, the magickal arts, divination, and water. Use blue or blue-green candles carved with the image of a wave to invoke him.

- **Erzulie** (Haitian): A protective goddess of love. One of her colors is blue, and any watery aromas are suited to her worship.

- **Fortuna** (Roman): Goddess of fate. Her color is gold and her symbols include a wheel, sphere, or cornucopia.

❧ **Ganesa** (Hindu): God of luck, affluence, sagacity, and writing. Dab your candles with jasmine and decorate them with a quartz crystal.

❧ **Hathor** (Egyptian): Goddess of women, she embodies all female qualities. One of her colors is bronze, and her symbol is a cow. Dab your candles with rose or sandalwood oil to honor her.

❧ **Hiribi** (Hittite): A moon god who also embodies the abundant harvest. Honor him with white, silver, or harvest-colored wax.

❧ **Hypnos** (Greek): God of sleep. Honor him with dark colors (deep purple, midnight blue, black) or by carving a closed eye in the candle wax.

❧ **Indra** (Hindu): God of victory, battle, and rain. Use cedar as an aromatic or the image of a clover.

❧ **Iris** (Greek): Goddess of the rainbow. Her symbol is both the rainbow and staff. Find a multi-colored candle for her.

❧ **Kan** (Mayan): God of the East; his color is yellow. Place a yellow candle in the eastern quarter of your circle when invoking that direction's energy.

❧ **Kataragama** (Ceylon): A greater god whose color is red.

❧ **Kundalini** (Hindu): The feminine life force of the universe, ever shifting and changing. Her aroma is lotus and her color is iridescent or rainbow-hued.

❧ **Ma'at** (Egyptian): Goddess of the law and justice. Her color is red and her symbol is a feather.

❧ **Manabozoho** (Algonquin): God/hero who created writing and protects many arts. Place a pale yellow or pink candle for him in the East (similar to the colors at dawn).

❧ **Mari** (Basque): Supreme queen of heaven whose symbols are a horse or a sickle, and whose colors are white or rainbow hues.

ॐ **Mars** (Roman): God of war, courage, and victory. His color is red, his symbols include a sword, and his aromatic should be very powerful (like ginger). Use an iron candleholder when working with this energy.

ॐ **Meret** (Egyptian): Goddess of song and happiness; her color is gold.

ॐ **Mithras** (Persian): God of ethics, light, victory, and the sun. His color is gold.

ॐ **Murukan** (Hindu): A god of hunting and warrior energy, his color is red and his emblem is a cock or a spear.

ॐ **Neptune** (Roman): God of the sea and all that dwells therein (patron of sailors). Suitable candles include those made from gold, blue, or blue-green wax dabbed with myrrh and carved with the symbol of a fish.

ॐ **Nike** (Greek): Goddess of victory. One of her colors is emerald green, her scent is rose, and her symbol is a palm branch or a wing.

ॐ **Oannes** (Babylonian): God of wisdom. Use dark purple or blue candles to represent him, carved with the image of a fish.

ॐ **Odin** (Scandinavian): God of magick, muse, cleverness, and war. Honor him in the sacred space with a turquoise decorated candle dabbed with musk oil.

ॐ **P'an-ku** (Chinese): God of balance and order. Carve the image of an egg on your candle to honor him, or a yin-yang emblem.

ॐ **Papa** (Polynesian): Earth mother, whose colors are silver and gold. Use a sand candle to represent her.

ॐ **Quetzalcoatl** (Aztec): God of fertility, wisdom, practicality, knowledge, life, and the winds, he's often represented by a feather or a snake.

- **Ratnasambhava** (Chinese): God of the South and the season of spring, his color is yellow and his emblem is a lion or an upturned palm. Use spring aromatics to honor him (early blossoming flowers).

- **Sedna** (Alaskan): Goddess of food, represented by a finger, seals, whales, or bears. Her colors are usually dark in tone, as she is also associated with the underworld.

- **Sekhmet** (Egyptian): Lion goddess who presides over divine order in all things. Her color is flame red or gold (like the sun). Dab your candles with beer or pomegranate juice to honor her.

- **Shekinah** (Hebrew): Goddess of wisdom. Her color is flame red and she can be represented by a candle's flame.

- **Shou-Hsing** (Chinese): God of longevity. His colors are white and pale pink, and his aroma is peach.

- **Sin** (Chaldean): God of wisdom, time, the calendar, and the moon. His color is lapis blue.

- **Thab-Iha** (Tibetan): A hearth god whose color is red and whose symbol is a snake held aloft. Use culinary spices as incense or candle dressing.

- **Tyr** (Teutonic): God of law. He may be represented by an upward pointing candle carved into a red candle.

- **Uto** (Egyptian): An ancient goddess who represents the vital earth and it's regenerative energy. Her color is green and her emblem is a snake. Use woodsy aromatics.

- **Vishnu** (Hindu): A Vedic sun god whose colors include blue and yellow. Suitable symbols to carve into a candle include a shell or mace, dabbed with lotus oil.

- **White Woman** (Honduran): Goddess of beauty, her colors are white and silver, and her symbol is a bird.

- ✤ **Xochipilli** (Aztec): God of love, spring, dance, music, and youthful outlooks. Honor him with floral scented candles on the seventh hour of any day.

- ✤ **Yakushi Nyorai** (Japanese): God who heals. Honor him with carvings of the sun or moon on your candles along with healing aromatics.

- ✤ **Yemaja** (Nigerian): Goddess of seas, rivers, and lakes; her color is blue. A cresting wave of the zodiac sign of Cancer can represent her.

- ✤ **Yu-Ti** (Chinese): A chief deity who presides over the sky and is a creator. His color is gold or any shade of jade. Use clay candleholders to honor him.

Another way to use candles in association with the Divine is by having a candle that symbolizes any one of a number of gods/goddesses under whose dominion fire light comes. Any being who controlled fire light would also be able to empower and bless your candle-burning efforts and give them a boost. Following is a brief list of just some of the world's gods/goddesses who had some connection with fire light.

Gods and Goddesses of Fire Light

- ✤ **A-ba-sei** (Chinese): Presides over hearth fires and is represented by a three-legged stove.

- ✤ **Agin deo** (Indian): A fire god by whom oaths are sworn.

- ✤ **Agni** (Balinese, Indian): Abides in fires of offering or worship, and protects the home and its prosperity.

- ✤ **Ayaba** (Dahomey): Goddess of the kitchen fires and food; she can be invoked with a candle at the dinner or kitchen table.

- ✤ **Bastet** (Egyptian): Goddess of warm, fertile flames, represented by a cat.

ॐ **Brigindo** (Celtic): Goddess of fire who also inspires poetic efforts.

ॐ **Brigit** (Irish): Goddess of all sacred fires, particularly those of hearth and home. Brigit is known as a healer and guardian of various arts.

ॐ **Chih Ching-tzu** (Chinese): The personification of spiritual fire, which candles represent.

ॐ **Gabija** (Lithuanian): Fire and hearth goddess who protects the family. She is best represented by an ever-burning candle (to put this out extinguishes love in the home).

ॐ **Gibil** (Assyrian): Fire and healing god who purifies us and watches over all forms of symbolic magick, which includes candle-burning efforts.

ॐ **Glut** (Scandinavian): Wife of Loki, her name means "glow." Her daughters were Eisa (embers) and Einmyria (ashes).

ॐ **Hestia** (Greek): Goddess of household fires and purity.

ॐ **Ho Shen** (Chinese): Fire god whose temples are often used by fortunetellers. Might be suited to candle-divination efforts.

ॐ **Huchi** (Japanese): Goddess who oversees domestic fires and protects those within the home from sickness. Best invoked with candlelit prayers.

ॐ **Hwa Kwang** (Taoist): God of light, specifically the soul's fire and light. Also abides in the fire of oil lamps (an alternative candle).

ॐ **Ixcozauhqui** (Aztec): God of fire who watches over the year's progression. Very suited to honoring birthdays.

ॐ **Kefeliu** (Peublo): Old woman of the fire, especially those of the home and sacred ritual spaces.

ॐ **Maui Motu'a** (Polynesian): Guardian of fire.

ॐ **Me-lha** (Tibetaan): Fire god who drives away evil spirits.

∾ **Memdeye-Ecie** (Siberian): Father of fire; abides in the East (dawn).

∾ **Mo-bo-sei** (Chinese): Fire god who keeps all flames from damaging homes.

∾ **Nairyosangha** (Iranian): A fire god who acts as a messenger between the worlds, specifically between the gods and humans.

∾ **Okitsuhime** (Japanese): Goddess of the kitchen and hearth fire.

∾ **Ot** (Siberian): A kindly fire goddess who protects relationships, especially marriage.

∾ **Pahpobi Kwiyo** (New Mexican): This goddess' name means fire flower, and she embodies the supernatural fires (magickal, spiritual).

∾ **Pattini** (southern Indian): Goddess who is the source of all fires.

∾ **Phloeng** (Thai): The spirit of fire that is sometimes invoked during childbirth.

∾ **Phoroneus** (Greek): Fire giver and the fire itself.

∾ **Safa** (Caucasian): Goddess of the hearth, by whom promises are made.

∾ **Sakhala** (Siberian): The goddess who rules all fires.

∾ **Suci** (Indian): The purifying, cleansing fires.

∾ **Tatevali** (Mexican): God of life and health-giving fires who also presides over herbs and prophesy. Represented by eagles and tigers.

∾ **Thab-lha** (Tibetan): Hearth god who aids with financial matters.

∾ **Togo Musun** (Siberian): Fire mistress who protects the family, clan, or greater tribe.

- **Vesta** (Roman): Goddess of sacred fires, public fires, and household fires, especially those with continuous flames.
- **Xaaceszini** (Navaho): God who represents effective control over the fire element.
- **Xiuhtecuhtli** (Aztec): God who watches over the universe's fires, best honored during the first hour of night or morning.

Just one word of advice in using either one of these correspondence lists: Don't call on a specific god or goddess without first establishing a relationship with him or her and understanding the cultural setting in which this image appears. Just as you wouldn't just go knock on a complete stranger's door and ask for something personal, the same holds true with the faces of the gods and goddesses.

৵৽৵৽৵৽

We need to respect what each of these names represents in the greater scheme of things, and to gently honor our relationship with the Divine in our magick. Candle-lighting can help us do that, but more so our attitude and hearts need to be in the right place. When they are, zap! There's the magick!

Appendix
Candle Tips and Terms

I n your candle-burning magick and candle-making efforts you may come up against various situations that leave you befuddled, like how the heck to get wax out of carpeting and special fabrics! This is quite common. So, I've assembled a list of helps and hints here that should make things a little easier. Additionally, at the end of this Appendix you'll find a list of candle terms that will help you better select the components for your candle-making and burning efforts.

Cleaning Up

℞ If a candle drips on fabric, always let it cool before trying to remove it. Place a piece of paper over the top of a cooled wax spill. Press this very gently using an iron on low setting. Remove the paper as it absorbs the wax. If this doesn't work, run the fabric under boiling water (not into a sink or your sink will clog).

 ᔢ Another way to get wax off fabric is by freezing it and removing small bits at a time, followed by the above process.
 ᔢ When candles are dirty from lying being stored, rubbing them with a soft cloth dabbed with olive oil cleans them up nicely.
 ᔢ Votive candle holders clean up more readily if you put a little water in the base beforehand.

Rituals and Gatherings

 ᔢ Lighting a candle once before an event and then blowing it out will make lighting easier.
 ᔢ Keep the candles out of drafts to avoid having them blow out or drip excessively. If this is impossible, use candles that have some protection against drafts (such as pillar candles).
 ᔢ Refrigerate candles before use (wrap them in aluminum foil or plastic wrap first). This helps the wax burn longer and more evenly.
 ᔢ If an aromatic candle has lost its oomph just before a spell or ritual, dab it with a little essential oil, moving from the bottom up, to build the best possible energy. You can reverse this motion for banishing spells.

Safety

By far, candle safety is one of the most important things you can observe. After all, ours is to "harm none," including ourselves, and no one wants to have precious items burned away in a candle-ignited fire. To help, please judiciously follow these guidelines:

 ᔢ Keep candles away from curtains, hair, and other flammable items.
 ᔢ Never leave a burning candle unattended.
 ᔢ Cup the flame of a candle with your hand when blowing it out. You won't have to blow as hard, and this in turn keeps wax from splattering.
 ᔢ Keep candles away from drafts, and keep their wicks well trimmed (not to exceed a 1/4 inch before burning).

৯০ Try not to let candles burn down past 2 inches above the rim of their holders. This is especially important if you're using wooden candle holders!

Storage

Living in a four-season climate, I often forget that candle wax isn't as forgiving of temperature changes as I am! If you don't want limp or misshapen candles, follow these guidelines:

৯০ Keep candles in a cool (under 70 degrees), dark area. This preserves both the color and aroma.

৯০ Keep differently scented candles separated from one another in storage or they'll absorb each other's aromas.

৯০ Wrap candles individually so they maintain their aromas.

৯০ Lay candles flat so they don't bend out of shape if the temperature goes up unexpectedly.

৯০ At a camping event, keep candles in a cooler to protect them.

৯০ Keep differently colored candles separated with wrapping paper. This will keep the colors from bleeding into each other.

Candle Terminology

Just for fun, here are some of the common terms applied to candles. You may find this helpful when looking for the right candle for a spell or ritual, or components with which to make a particular type of candle.

Cast candle: Also called a molded candle. The wax for these candles gets poured into a predetermined shape (for example, milk carton candles often made by children). Molds can be made easily or purchased at craft shops.

Container candle: A candle whose wax is poured directly into the container that will hold it while burning. Long-burning candles are often made this way for greater safety and less dripping.

Dipped Candle: Made by a very time-consuming process in which a wick is dipped into melted wax repeatedly. This is how taper candles are made.

Drawn Candle: This doesn't create a candle per se, but an over-waxed wick, which was popular in some older types of lamps. This is also a method of making tiny candles, like those for a birthday cake. Slowly draw a long length of wick through wax to allow it to collect a heavy covering of wax.

Extruded Candles: A mechanically created candle that's produced by pushing wax through a template, like one might squeeze icing onto a cake, and then cutting it to specific sizes.

Novelty candles: Just about every type of candle that doesn't fit into a pat description, such as ones shaped like animals or people. Novelty candles often work very well as poppets.

Pillar candle: Pillar candles have a geometrical cross section. In buying pillar candles or equipment be aware that they are described by *diameter*, not height. For example, a 4-inch pillar would be 4 inches across a circle, square, or octagon, depending upon the mold used.

Poured Candle: An old method of building up a candle by repeatedly pouring wax over the wick. Similar to dipped candles, these can result in different shapes.

Pressed Candle: A modern method of making candles from wax beads.

Rolled Candles: This is a wonderfully easy method of candle-making that uses sheets of wax that get rolled around a wick. A little heat at the end of the sheet secures it in place.

Taper: These are the most common kind of candle, with a 7/8-inch diameter on average, and a length of 5 to 9 inches.

Votive candles: Also known as tea candles, these are tiny round candles that fit into glass or other containers. They are usually not more than 1 1/2 inches across and 3 inches high. Tea candles are typically smaller than most votives.

Wick: A braided piece of cord treated with mordant (pickling) that's lit to burn the candle. The mordant regulates how quickly or slowly the wick burns. Different types of wicks are covered in Chapter 1.

Select Bibliography

Aldington, Richard, trans. *New Larousse Encyclopedia of Mythology*. Middlesex, England: Hamlyn Publishing, 1973.

Ann, Martha, and Dorothy Myers Imel. *Goddesses in World Mythology*. New York: Oxford University Press, 1995.

Beyerl, Paul. *Herbal Magick*. Custer, Wash.: Phoenix Publishing, 1998.

Bruce-Mitford, Miranda. *Illustrated Book of Signs and Symbols*. New York: DK Publishing, 1996.

Budge, E.A. Wallis. *Amulets and Superstitions*. Oxford, England: Oxford University Press, 1930.

Cavendish, Richard. *A History of Magic*. New York: Taplinger Publishing, 1979.

Cristiani, R.S. *Perfumery and Kindred Arts*. Baird and Company, Philadelphia: 1877.

Cunningham, Scott. *Encyclopedia of Magical Herbs*. St. Paul: Llewellyn Publications, 1988.

———. *Magic in Food*. St. Paul: Llewellyn Publications, 1991.

————. *Crystal, Gem, and Metal Magic*. St. Paul: Llewellyn Publications, 1995.

Davison, Michael Worth, ed. *Everyday Life Through the Ages*. Pleasantville, N.Y.: Reader's Digest Association, 1992.

Farrar, Jane and Stewart *Spells and How They Work*. Phoenix, Wash., 1990.

Freethy, Ron. *Book of Plant Uses, Names, and Folklore*. New York: Tanager Books, 1985.

Gordon, Leslie: *Green Magic*. New York: Viking Press, 1977.

Gordon, Stuart. *Encyclopedia of Myths and Legends*. London: Headline Book Publishing, 1993.

Hall, Manley P. *Secret Teachings of All Ages*. Philosophical Research Society, Los Angeles: 1977.

Hutchinson, Ruth. *Everyday's a Holiday*. New York: Harper and Brothers, 1961.

Kunz, George Frederick. *Curious Lore of Precious Stones*. New York: Dover Publications, 1971.

Leach, Maria, ed. *Standard Dictionary of Folklore, Mythology, and Legend*. New York: Harper and Row, 1984.

Loewe, Michael, and Carmen Blacker, eds. *Oracles and Divination*. Boulder: Shambhala, 1981.

Miller, Gastavus Hindman. *Ten Thousand Dreams Interpreted*. Chicago: M.A. Donohuse and Co., 1931.

Mitford, Miranda Bruce. *Illustrated Book of Signs and Symbols*. New York: DK Publishing, 1996.

Opie, Iona, and Moira Tatem. *A Dictionary of Superstitions*. New York: Oxford University Press, 1989.

Oppenheimer, Betty. *The Candlemaker's Companion*. Pownal, Vt.: Storey Books, 1997.

Potterton, D., ed. *Culpeper's Herbal.* New York: Sterling Publishing, 1983.

Telesco, Patricia. *Kitchen Witch's Cookbook.* St. Paul: Llewellyn Publications, 1994.

———. *The Language of Dreams.* Freedom, Calif.: Crossing Press, 1997.

———. *Futuretelling.* Freedom, Calif.: Crossing Press, 1997.

———. *Herbal Arts.* Secaucus, N.J.: Citadel Books, 1997.

Walker, Barbara. *The Woman's Dictionary of Symbols and Sacred Objects.* San Francisco: Harper and Row, 1988.

Waring, Philippa. *The Dictionary of Omens and Superstitions.* Secaucus, N.J.: Chartwell Books, 1978.

Index

About the Author

P atricia Telesco is a mother of three, wife, chief human to five pets, and full-time professional author with more than 50 metaphysical books on the market. These include *Goddess in My Pocket, Futuretelling, The Herbal Arts, Kitchen Witch's Cookbook, Little Book of Love Magic, Your Book of Shadows, Spinning Spells: Weavng Wonders,* and other diverse titles, each of which represents a different area of spiritual interest for her and her readers.

Trish considers herself a down-to-earth, militant, wooden-spoon—wielding Kitchen Witch whose love of folklore and worldwide customs flavor every spell and ritual. Although her original Wiccan education was self-trained and self-initiated, she later received initiation into the Strega tradition of Italy, which gives form and fullness to the folk magick Trish practices. Her strongest beliefs lie in following personal vision, being tolerant of other traditions, making life an act of worship, and being creative so that magick grows with you.

Trish travels twice a month to give lectures and workshops around the country. She has appeared on several television segments, including one for *Sightings* on muli-cultural divination systems, and one for the *Debra Duncan Show* on modern Wicca. Trish also maintains a strong presence in metaphysical journals, including *Circle Network News* and *Silver Chalice*, and on the Internet through such popular sites as *www.witchvox.com* (festival focus), her Web site at *www.loresinger.com*, her Yahoo! club at *www.clubs.yahoo.com/clubs/folkmagicwithtrishtelesco*, and appearances on Internet chats and bulletin boards.

Trish's hobbies include gardening, herbalism, brewing, singing, handcrafts, antique restoration, and landscaping. Her current project is helping to coordinate spiritually centered tours to Europe, including a ghost and fairy tour of Ireland in 2002. She is also actively involved in promoting and supporting pagan land funds so we have more spaces to gather and worship freely. See *www.phoenixfestivals.com* and *www.dragonhills.com* for more information.